Dollars & Sense

Also by T. L Sacristen

Make Money Make Money

Dollars & Sense

T. L. Sacristen

iUniverse, Inc.
New York Lincoln Shanghai

Dollars & Sense

iUniverse books may be ordered through booksellers or by contacting:

iUniverse
2021 Pine Lake Road, Suite 100
Lincoln, NE 68512
www.iuniverse.com
1-800-Authors (1-800-288-4677)

ISBN-13: 978-0-595-28134-3
ISBN-10: 0-595-28134-6

Printed in the United States of America

state to the latter. Best of all they are well written and eminently reliable, entertaining even. Read. Enjoy. And Profit. You'll be glad you did.

Norma Williamson, Communications Instructor
Author, Monday People

◆　　◆　　◆

...articles on financial matters...extremely informative. They have provided...up-to-date information...useful in my financial planning. I would recommend...to all who are concerned about their financial matters or retirement.

Richard D. Koshel, Dean, Professor of Physics

◆　　◆　　◆

Financial planning can be very intimidating so we procrastinate...delay financial planning...not understand its importance...wait until near retirement...how much money they will need?
...provides easy-to-read examples and descriptions of financial terms and actions that simplify financial planning. I encourage you to read this book and begin financial planning, now.

John E. Ford, Professor Communications

Contents

Section Three Retirement Planning

Section Four Estate Planning

Section Five Odds & Ends

Acknowledgements

Like the turtle on a fence post, I've had help. This book has benefited from talents of many and I thank them.

Time and advice from professionals and business owners is credited with extending the reach of this book far beyond my personal limitations. Although they have counseled and advised, responsibility for any oversight is mine alone.

I name names at great peril of embarrassing omissions. However, Vernon Ammon, Professor of Plant Pathology; Denzil Causey, Attorney and CPA; Henry J. Donaghy, Professor of English; Donald R. Epley, MIA, SRA, Professor of Real Estate & Finance; Carole & Jim Gilliam, Insurance & Real Estate; Robert Hershbarger, CLU, Professor of Insurance; Martin F. Jue, President, MFJ Enterprises, Richard D. Koshel, Professor of Physics; Barry Montgomery, Retailer, and William Ward, Attorney have freely advised. There are far too many others to name so I must be content with dedicating this book to:

To friends and clients
who have taught me much
and that I still have a lot to learn.
And to my family
in thanks for not abandoning me
when I was very young,
and knew everything.

Author's Preface

When you are rich, you are witty, you are wise and you sing well too. Hebrew Proverb, and perhaps reason enough to be rich.

The purpose of this book is to help those who save to increase the rewards of their virtue. To that end *Dollars & Sense* offers money management basics in language light and plain. So much as possible the arcane jargon of finance is avoided. Within the limits of my ability, the text is straightforward and easy to read. Strange words, or common words used strangely, are italicized and *glossarized*.

Financial planning is mostly judgement and common sense, the art/science of making best compromise from conflicting objectives. While I have worked hard to make this text accurate and reliable, opinions are a part of this book. Opinions are always drawn from imperfect information. Good answers to most financial planning questions will usually be a matter of judgement; hopefully, in this book readers will discover ways, means and methods to help them form more accurate opinions and better judgements.

What readers should expect is easy to understand explanations of basic financial tools and techniques. Financial products are broken down to essential functions. Uses, advantages and disadvantages are spelled out in ordinary language. My intent is to write so readers will understand the basics of instruments such as a Charitable Remainder Trust or Mutual Funds with two minutes easy reading.

This could be called a get rich slow book. It is devoted to the patient discipline of building and conserving wealth through sound planning and wise investment. Those totally averse to this approach should put this book aside until life has conditioned them for its methods.

Opportunities to speculate for quick profits will turn up, and they should be examined, but get expert advice, then move carefully. If there is high return potential, there is also high risk. There's nothing wrong with risk, just go carefully into that good deal and be prepared to take a loss. Homer put it more succinctly three thousand years ago:

How cautious are the wise.

Readers Should Not Expect ways to make zillions in real estate in twenty-five minutes. How to get two-hundred per-cent return, guaranteed. Instant-wealth-without-risk. This book does not deal in such nonsense. Get-rich-quick makes exciting reading but usually offers little of practical value. More often readers just get silly ideas and bad advice.

◆　　　◆　　　◆

How many times have we asked, *If I only knew then…?* It is said, *Everyone learns from experience, but the wise learn from the experience of others.* For twenty-odd years my clients and I have worked through good and bad marriages, successful and failed divorces, career changes, retirements and enough mid-life crises to support a psychologist with a spending fetish. Readers are offered that *experience of others* from many lifetimes.

Because my primary occupation is helping people accumulate and manage money, because I write and give talks about money, readers may assume I believe money to be of transcending importance. Let us put this notion to rest. *Love People, Use Money.* That old saw puts money in proper perspective. People and relationships are important, money much less so. Money is merely a tool; however, it is an important tool and using it well creates freedom and more options. Greater freedom and more options makes life easier and a lot more fun. And, while we're here, life's better if we have a good time.

My observations while working with folks in all life's stages, from youngsters with nothing but dreams to those who've made it happen, convinces me money does not bring happiness. Often, the opposite is true. Happiness or satisfaction seems to come almost exclusively from fulfillment of personal ambitions and being able to manage life on one's own terms. Meeting personal goals and challenges usually brings financial success, but the personal wealth and independence that typically come with attaining worthwhile objectives seem merely incidental. My experience confirms author Stuart Woods's stated belief that, *The Secret of happiness is finding a way to make a living doing the things you like best.*

This ad hoc theory seems to be supported by surveys of commissioned salespeople. These surveys show the top ten per-cent of commissioned salespeople make ninety percent of the money. Although those heavy-hitters make big bucks, they rank making a lot of money eighth in a list of ten personal objectives.

So, it seems happiness is much more than money and that making a lot of money appears to be mostly a side effect of succeeding in worthwhile personal ambitions. However, though money may not be the sum of all dreams, as Dolly Levi tells us in Hello Dolly, The difference between a little money and a lot is not *much, but the difference between no money and a little money is a lot. And,* common sense tells us it's not easy to be happy when one's got nothing in a world of plenty.

So, my advice is to make your living doing something you like. If you are not doing what you like, start looking around. Life is not a practice run and it's tough enough on the best of terms. If you don't like what you're doing, odds are you can find an occupation where you will be happier, healthier and ultimately wealthier in greater and lesser ways.

This may be is a bad idea, but here it is. Parts of this book are dull as my high school coach's civics class. Although I have attempted to lighten up insurance and annuities, to make them interesting even, it seems my best efforts fell short. However, there's some really dull financial stuff you really need to know. Dull stuff that is essential to sound financial planning. So, I suggest you read the portions that you find interesting, *entertaining even,* as Norma Williamson said to my delight, and then keep this book on your reference shelf. Do not torture yourself with the mind-numbing parts until you need to know about things like Variable Universal Life and Indexed Annuities. Trust me though, if you're lucky someday you'll accumulate assets and knowing that dull stuff will make or save you money. And, *making or saving you money is what this book is about.*

My Bona Fides

My professional designations include Chartered Financial Consultant, Chartered Life Underwriter and Life Underwriter Training Council Fellow. Additionally, I completed the Met Life Advanced Underwriting Advisor Program and spent two years working with top agents on business and estate planning cases. In a prior career, I graduated from the Sears Management Training Program and worked six years as a manager with full profit and loss responsibility.

Plaques dress up a wall, but the important stuff is not made of certificates, credentials or diplomas. For me, the more meaningful lessons came from working with outstanding professionals and business owners. My thinking on management, enterprise and lifestyle has been honed by decades of exposure to talented and thoughtful people from many walks of life.

Mostly, I'm a salesman. I've sold bibles, newspapers, encyclopedias, appliances, insurance, stocks and bonds, mutual funds, real estate…you get the idea. I continue to sell. It's fun. Selling anything one believes in can be a great way to make a living, but the best adventures come from selling ideas. Ideas are tops because selling ideas is more challenging. It no big deal to sell something a buyer can see, touch, and lust after, but getting others to buy an idea, now that's a real challenge. I've got some ideas to sell here, if you buy some of them, I believe I've done good.

We are told failure is instructive. I would add that repeated failure is enlightening. For me life has been enlightening. My business education started early. At age eleven I failed as a paperboy, learning at that tender age that even friends may require supervision. Another venture taught me the hard way that things are not always what they seem and what you see is not always what you get. Another enterprise forcefully demonstrated what Charles Dickens[1] so amusingly implied and Clarence Darrow said outright, *"There is no justice, in or out of court."*

Contracts are only as good as those who make them. Confucius said, *Good government is possible only when good people are in government.* I'll bet he also said, *contracts are good only when made by good people,* and we just didn't hear about it. If a contract must be enforced by a court of law the game will probably *not be worth the candle.* Rather than taking contract breakers to court, it is often more prudent to just eat your losses and move on. Experience has made me more comfortable when deal makers look me in the eye as they shake my hand than when everybody signs reams of obtusely written contracts.

One of my more instructive failures. When I started at Sears, they promised if I finished their management training program and worked with them twenty years they'd make me rich. Maybe so, but I jumped ship before getting rich and started a video movie business. After all I had good management experience and what Sears claimed was the equalavent of an MBA. I quickly got a lot richer in experience and much poorer of purse.

---

1.   Bleak House, Charles Dickens A Civil Action, Jonathan Harr

Over the last several years we have seen a virtual deluge of new financial products. These products and rules for their use have generated such a flow of data that golden opportunities for improving financial performance are easily lost in the flood. This book can help readers find, evaluate and use ideas that might otherwise go unnoticed.

In these pages, conventional wisdom is frequently challenged. Rightly so. Conventional wisdom often lags decades behind reality, continuing to worship at the altar of outdated truisms long after their god is dead. We should respect traditional thinking, there is usually a good reason a line of thinking became traditional. However, we should also carefully examine any claim to superior method, idea or product. New ideas are often better, that's progress. Progress though, comes in fits and starts and rigid scrutiny should be a part of our examination of both the traditional and the innovative.

A little help with scrutiny.

The late Carl Sagan gave us "Baloney Detection." Michael Shermer more recently offered a similar construct in Scientific American. Bertran Russell also gave us some good clues. I borrow a bit from each of those apostles of clear thinking to posit the following aids to sorting wheat from chaff, gold from glitter and the purveyors of truth and wisdom from charlatans and mountebanks:

1. Is the source of the claim reliable?

2. Does source have a good record?

3. Can claims be verified?

4. Do claims stack up against what you know?

5. Has claim been challenged by competent authority?

    Bertrand Russell on skepticism.
    When experts are agreed,
    the opposite opinion cannot be held certain.
    When experts do not agree,
    no opinion can be held to be certain.

Will this book tell you everything you need to know about money and financial planning? No, of course not. I have worked and studied money matters for decades, but still must cope with things beyond my knowledge and experience.

While this is humbling, it nurtures a profound respect for my ignorance and keeps me aware of personal limitations. To put it another way, we don't know what we don't know. So, keep an open mind, but look both ways before crossing streets or venturing into new territory.

Thoreau said, *The mass of men lead lives of quiet desperation.* Unfortunately it seems this is still true, but today, it need not be. In times past most lived the life they were born to; but, times have changed. Today, more than ninety percent of *the successful* are making it on their own. Checking out the paths they took to their *success*, we usually find it blazed with educational landmarks.

The Overclass

The word *overclass* is making a place in our vocabulary. Overclass refers to an emerging group that commands very high incomes by combining skill or knowledge with willingness to work. A great thing about this newly defined class is that it makes no distinction of race, gender or age but,proffers membership solely on basis of skill and effort.

So if you would be successful, and probably make a lot of money, get a good education, then work smart at something you like. Today, more than ever before, knowledge and hard work can overcome real or perceived barriers and move one up the socioeconomic ladder. We have entered the information age. In this age knowledge is golden.

Knowledge has always been valuable, but the increased facility with which it can now be exchanged has made it more marketable. As the past belonged to the landed aristocracy, the future belongs to the educated. And, after all…only the educated are free.—Epictetus

Working Money is not expected to be a tome of great significance. Such noble endeavor is beyond the reach of my humble ambition. My purpose here is merely to help those who spend less than they make to increase the rewards of their virtue. However, if by some chance this book should be widely read and cause great numbers to have higher returns on more savings thereby creating a greater capital base that increases our productivity, making the global marketplace more efficient and thereby improving the lot of all successive generations, I would be pleased to take a small measure of credit but hopefully, never, not ever start taking myself too seriously. T. L. Sacristen

Section One
Financial Planning

o o o o o o o o o o o o o o o o o o o o o o o o o o o o o o o o o

Race horse syndication.
A legitimate enterprise
but most of us would do better
to just buy the manure outright.

1

What is Financial Planning?

o o o o o o o o o o o o o o o o o o o o o o o o o o o o o o o o

"Young men dream—of being rich.
Rich men dream—of being young."

—Martin F. Jue
Everyone says, "Martin is the smartest man I've ever known."

Summary

The many dubious and confusing schemes pandered under the guise of financial planning have left consumers confused about financial planning and planners. Consumers often wonder, "What is Financial Planning?" The matter begs clarification. Financial planning is the act of organizing resources so objectives are accomplished efficiently.

1—Evaluate present situation. 2—Define objectives. 3—Make plans for meeting objectives. 4—Implement plan.

Getting people to do long term financial planning is like getting teen-agers to eat right and exercise, the need is there but not the motivation. Writes Ellen Schultz, in The Wall Street Journal.

Why is this true? Good planning is likely to double the rate at which an individual or family accumulates wealth and, at the same time it helps define and protect against risks to financial security. Given the importance of financial planning, why do most not have a long-range financial plan or even a budget? Volumes have been written but it boils down to this:

The first is time. Day-to-day activities can be all consuming and leave little time for nebulosities like long range financial planning. A second reason is uncertainty:

What *is* financial planning?

The term financial planning has been applied to everything from gold mines in Arkansas to race horse syndication. Now there was a gold mine in Arkansas, I have a prospectus. The prospectus is worth more than all the gold that came out of the mine. Race horse syndication? A legitimate enterprise, but most of us would do better to just buy the manure outright.

With all the confusing schemes and swindles pandered under the guise of financial planning its no wonder consumers are uncertain about financial planning and planners. The matter deserves clarification.

What *is* financial planning? Financial planning is the act of organizing resources so objectives are accomplished efficiently. It is a four-step process.

1. Evaluate present situation. Review income, expenses, savings and investments.

2. Define objectives. Set priorities and timelines. Be specific and realistic. For example. Monthly retirement income of $5000 might be a long-term goal.

3. Develop a plan to meet yours goals. Retirement income of $5000 monthly is a retirement goal. Income from pension and Social Security will be $3500. Determine how to make up the remaining $1500.

4. Implement plan.

You now know where you are, where you want to go and how to get there. Just do it. The longest journey begins with step one. Not quite the Chinese proverb. The Financial Data Sheet at end of this section can help.

Financial Planners: Who Needs Them?

Now that we've cleared up what financial planning *is*, what about financial planners? In the early eighties financial planning became a buzzword. Overnight it seemed the world's cup was run over and badly bent by uncounted numbers of *financial planners*. The now defunct A. L. Williams & Associates appointed thousands of "financial planners." Most were in and out of the business in a matter of weeks and the influx and outgo of these pretenders created the attitudes that spawned the joke where wife says to husband, *Honey, your financial planner just delivered my pizza.*

Anyone who dealt with money, finance or insurance suddenly became a *Financial Planner.* Most states have no regulations governing who may *hold themselves out* as financial planners and many do who are no way qualified. At the same time many new *financial planners* were hanging out shingles, the term financial planning was tacked onto many dubious activities and, virtually every outright swindle coming down the pike. It got so bad bona fide financial planners and consultants began to shy away from these descriptive titles. As a matter of practice, almost every insurance agent, stockbroker, banker or accountant does some financial planning. It goes with the territory, and there are many conscientious professionals in these fields who hold no formal credentials.

Most in the money business are honest, competent folk doing the right things well. However, there are though enough goniffs, mountebanks and financially challenged klutzes in the mix to justify alertness. I do not call for regulation; regulation usually helps little and costs like rip, but I do importune, *buyer beware, buyer be informed. Trust, but verify.*

In recent years, the volume of data created by our dealings has increased at an exponential rate and even the best informed among us sometimes need help negotiating the information superhighway. Most of us have difficulty keeping abreast of our own specialty, let alone finding time or energy to become expert in other complex fields. Like every other specialty the financial world has grown increasingly complex. More powerful computers enable financial services companies to collect and process data with unprecedented speed. And with all this data comes new products and news ways to use them. Constant change in tax rules further complicates matters and makes going it alone more difficult. The value of doing the right thing and, the cost of not knowing are off the charts. It is usually the better part of wisdom to seek professional help.

When you are ready, where do you find a financial planner? Ask around. Someone you know can probably recommend one. Word of mouth still works pretty well. Back to the net and or, let your fingers do the walking, look under Financial Consultants, Financial Planners. Ask for references and if they are provided, check them out. If they are not provided, be wary.

Plan on a meeting or two with prospective planners. Keep in mind that when you find *the* financial planner you are looking for a long and intimate relationship. You will, at least you should, tell them everything. Things you haven't told your lawyer, your spouse or your mother will come out in discussions of your money, your life, your hopes, dreams and regrets.

Financial planners, who needs them? Only those who deal with money, pensions contracts or taxes. Should you get professional help? Probably, but do some homework first. The more you take to the financial planning process, the more you will take away.

Finish this book. Then look to the Internet and the library for more.
Who is qualified to be your financial planner? The ChFC, Chartered Financial Consultant; CLU, Chartered Life Underwriter; CFP, Certified Financial Planner and CPAs with special training are nationally recognized financial planning designations. Additionally, many accountants, attorneys, bank officers, insurance agents and registered representatives have special training in financial planning. *No professional designation guarantees competence,* and there are good practitioners without formal designations; however, holders of recognized credentials have met established standards and must participate in continuing education programs.

Sound financial planning requires familiarity with taxation, insurance, investments, pensions and contracts. Obviously, no individual can master all these complex fields. Good financial planners are usually specialists in one area and have basic knowledge of others. Good planners enhance their expertise by networking with other specialists, so, be wary prima donnas presuming, or pretending, to *know it all.*

Wills & Living Trusts

No financial plan is complete without a Will or Living Trust to direct disposition of assets. Lack of such direction can cause hardship, delay and disposition of assets without consideration of owner's wishes. The primary difference between a Will and a Living Trust is that a Will is subject to oversight by a *Probate Court* and a Living Trust is not.

It is a common misconception that avoidance of probate reduces tax obligations. *Avoiding Probate Court does not effect tax liabilities.* Convenience, privacy and speed of execution may make Living Trusts appropriate but they do not reduce taxes. With small estates where special situations exist, where minor children are involved for example, probate court oversight may be desirable.

2

So You Want to be Rich

o o o o o o o o o o o o o o o o o o o o o o o o o o o o o o o o o o o o o o
"With money in your pocket you are witty, you are wise, and you sing well too."

—*Yiddish Proverb, and perhaps reason enough to be rich.*

Summary

Rich for most of us is a matter of definition. To me Rich is when with my money working, I don't need to. For most, getting rich is simply a matter of spending less than you make. A matter discipline: saving a meaningful portion of earnings and investing prudently will make one rich. Making and keeping a commitment to a savings plan is far more important than where the savings are invested. Put it in the nest egg first, then budget the rest. Being rich is having choices. Spend less than you make and there will come a time when you have the option to work at what you wish when you wish and, to play when you want. That kind of freedom requires a nest egg approximately twenty times annual income needs.

Don Eply, professor of finance recently shared with me three paths to riches that will work for anyone. Being a generous sort, I pass them along. *"Win the Lottery. Inherit, or spend less than you make."* We have little control over the first two so let's have a closer look at method number three. But first, let's define rich. Rich is relative, and largely a matter of who defines it. Your definition will almost certainly be different, but here's mine.

To me, rich is when your money's working you don't need to. At least you don't need to work for a living. There are, of course, better reasons than need for working.

So, by my definition, rich means a principal sum equal to about twenty times annual income needs, or wants. That amount prudently invested will likely provide inflation adjusted life income from a growing principal.

Spending less than you make, how long does it take to be rich? That of course depends on how much less you spend than you make. Wisely investing to ten per-cent of gross income should do the job in about twenty-seven years. At fifteen per-cent, plan on twenty.

Most folks aren't satisfied with that time frame. They complain that with this method they will be a lot older before they are rich. No doubt, but with any luck they'll be older, rich or not, so they may as well take the sure road to riches, and meanwhile dream of one and two.

Still, most want to get rich quick. Nothing wrong with that, but although most get-rich-quick schemes may leave us richer in experience, all too often we become poorer of purse. I can say that with authority, I'm pretty rich in experience myself.

Sometimes though an opportunity comes along that just can't miss. These should be examined, but go carefully and get another opinion; even a gift horse can run up a vet bill.

A good friend and client, a professional man, was making good progress, but after several years on the sure and steady road he got impatient, started looking for hot deals. He found one. A can't miss, hush-hush, limited offer on shares of a gold mine in Arkansas. His cousin told him about it. Hope he got kissed. He said he didn't talk to me because, *I was sure you would try to talk me out of it.* After his wife left him, my good friend moved out west somewhere, but he's richer in experience.

Found my own hot deal, not so long ago. A client company invented a new process. Their revolutionary new method would cut production costs almost in half and they were expanding to make more from their new advantage. They were selling stock to fund the expansion. I borrowed on AMEX and MasterCard to buy more than was prudent.

Come to find out the idea was not so new and someone else held the patent on the revolutionary process. A negotiated settlement. I took a bath, but gained experience.

Before we get into the next chapter where we'll discuss ways to figure how much one will need to save to get rich, this seems a good time to look at the *Rule of 72.* And, debt versus savings.

The Rule of 72, also called the *Compound Interest Rule,* tells us that if we take the number 72 and divide by the compound interest rate the result will equal the years needed for principal to double. 72 divided by 8 = 9. Yield of 8% compounded will double principal in 9 years. Or at 10%, (78/10) in 7.2 years. The Rule of 72 can be inverted to estimate future costs, for example: A car costs $20,000 today: If the price increases at 7.2% annually, an equivalent car will cost $40,000 after ten years.

The rule of 72 is a fine tool for quickly estimating the *time value of money* and *inflation's toll.* Both important financial planning considerations.

Another tidbit before we move on. We're often told it makes little difference whether we save money to buy something or buy it now and pay off the debt. It works out about the same and we might as well use it while we pay, right? Wrong, it makes a big difference.

If we borrow $10,000 at 8% and pay off the note in 120 monthly installments, payments will be $121.33. If we put $121.33 per month for 120 months into a Roth IRA yielding 8%, we will have $22,196.84 after 120 installments. Savings grow faster than debt is reduced because interest on borrowed amount must be paid before any of payment is applied against what is owed. When we save or invest, principal *and interest* earn interest.

I do not ever want to leave the impression I believe money to be of transcending importance. To the contrary, it won't make anyone happy. It has been my observation that the most likely distinction between the happy and the unhappy is education. Education creates awareness and appreciation of surroundings which enriches life in ways money can't. Money is nice. It opens doors and smoothes the path, but education is more fulfilling. Education is an investment that can't lose, and it pays great dividends.

3

Insurance & Risk Management

◆

Insurance: Managing Risk
Avoid-Assume-Share or Insure

○ ○

Heisenberg Uncertainty Principle: *a principle in quantum mechanics; it is impossible to discern simultaneously and with a high accuracy both the position and the momentum of a particle.*
Or, we might say—it is hard to be sure.

Summary

Insurance is about managing risk. Some risks we can avoid, some we can prudently assume, others we should share or insure. Managing risks well means making prudent decisions about whether to avoid, assume, share or insure risks. A risk can be shared or transferred by paying another party, usually by paying an insurance company, a fee or premium to assume all or part of a risk. Risk is endemic to life and business. Successful management of risk is important to both. Evaluating risk is critical to its management.

It will cost less to avoid or assume a risk than to insure it. When we pay an insurance company to take a risk, the insurance company must collect enough premium to cover actual losses, pay administrative expenses, and make a profit.

11

When we assume risk, we pay only actual losses and avoid those other expenses. However it is often wise to bear the greater cost of insuring a risk because while chance loss may be small, the loss could be devastating.

The first step in risk management is to decide if a risk can be avoided, can be assumed, should be shared or covered by insurance.

1—Is the risky activity essential?
2—Can risky activity be modified to eliminate or reduce risk to acceptable levels?
3—Can the risk be shared?

If the activity is essential, and cannot be modified or shared so as to reduce risk to tolerable levels, then the risk should be insured.

A good example of assumed, shared and insured risk is a Major Medical health insurance policy. Small bills are the responsibility of policy owner, the insurance company and policy owner share costs up to a stated larger amount, and the insurance company pays excess above that stipulated amount. For example:

A typical policy might have a $1,000 **deductible**, pay 80% of next $5,000 and 100% of remaining **covered** medical expense up to $1,000,000. With this policy, on a $10,000 claim, the insured would pay the $2,000. The $1,000 deductible, plus 20% of the next $5,000.

In this example:

Policyowner assumes risk for first $1000.
Policyowner pays insurance company to share risk for next $4000.
Policyowner pays insurance company to assume risk in excess of $5000. Such policies allow buyers to assume risks they can handle while protecting them against unaffordable losses. With Medical Insurance, as with most insurance policies, the buyer is offered a wide range of choices or deductibles so coverage can be adapted to individual needs.

4

Insurance

o o o o o o o o o o o o o o o o o o o o o o o o o o o o o o o o o o o

Insurance lets us live with the possibility of the unmanageable, even the unthinkable.

Summary

Life insurance provides for financial loss to family or business on the death of the insured. Health Insurance protects against medical bills that might be financially inconvenient or ruinous. Disability Income Insurance protects against loss of income because of illness or injury. Long-term Care policies protect against nursing home or assisted living costs. The protections offered by these specialized insurance forms are vital to successful financial plans. Insurance policies should explain benefits and limitations in plain language. Be wary of policies written in arcane jargon, the intent may be to obscure rather than to inform.

Life Insurance

Life insurance enables wage earners to provide for dependents in the event of a premature death. It also allows business owners to insure against loss of key persons and estate owners to guarantee cash will be available to pay taxes and facilitate equitable distribution of assets.

Life insurance uses are many and varied. Millions of pages have been written on the subject, but we're just going to hit high spots of the three primary uses, Family, Business and Estate Planning.

Obviously these uses overlap because families own businesses and often accumulate large estates. The distinctions blur, but for simplicity we will treat these life insurance situations separately.

Life insurance policy forms are covered in more detail in Chapter 13. The life insurance most frequently asked question, term or permanent, is also addressed in chapter 13.

Family Life Insurance

Is used to provide financial security for the family unit. Most often to replace income of a deceased wage earner. We start with the question, if a family member dies, will the family suffer a financial loss, and if so how much? If the answer is yes, the amount of the potential loss determines life insurance needed. When a wage earner dies, their income should be replaced, either for a period of time, or in perpetuity. It is usually sufficient to secure the lost income until the children are independent, but in some families it is desirable to provide permanent replacement of the lost income.

Estimate life insurance needed by calculating lost income. Then subtract Social Security benefits and income available from other sources. When you have an amount, multiply that amount by the years the income will be needed and discount for anticipated interest or investment earnings. It is wise to use conservative earnings estimates.

As a starting point, a principal sum equal to twenty times the amount needed annually, when prudently invested should yield permanent inflation adjusted income. Finite periods require lesser amounts.

For example:

John and Mary each net $30,000 annually. They have children Michael age 8 and Sally age 5. They have no savings or assets that could be converted to income.

Social Security benefits of roughly $12,000 annually would be paid to the family should either John or Mary die. That means the family would need to replace $18,000 income on death of either provider. John and Mary decide they would want enough life insurance to maintain family income in perpetuity.

The simple and conservative solution is, $30,000 minus $12,000 = $18,000 times 20 equals $360,000. $360,000 is needed on Mary and $360,000 is needed on John. Annual earnings of 5% on principle will equal $18,000. Once the sum needed for income is established, consider other needs, such as education funds, and decide if it is prudent increase basic life insurance to accommodate those requirements.

Life Insurance in Business

Business life insurance provides protection against deaths that could jeopardize company profits, stability or existence. The success of a business, especially a small business, often depends heavily on a few individuals, and premature death of those individuals could pose financial threats. Businesses frequently buy life insurance on those *Key Persons*. It is also common for partnerships and closely held corporations to buy life insurance on major stockholders to prevent owner-ship by inheritance from jeopardizing management and financial arrangements. Businesses also often use life insurance to supplement pensions and create *golden handcuffs* to tie key employees to the firm. Tax considerations usually play a major role in purchase of business life insurance and good idea to have counsel of a *CPA* and a Chartered Financial Consultant or Certified Financial Planner.

Life Insurance in Estate Planning

Large estates are often short of ready cash. Without careful planning inadequate liquidity can cause estate shrinkage by forcing inopportune sale of assets. Life insurance can provide cash for taxes and other settlement needs. Estates often include business interests that complicate distribution. Life insurance can provide cash to facilitate equitable distribution of estate assets without disrupting business ownership or management.

Health Insurance

Most families will want protection of a Major Medical Expense Policy. Such pol-icies usually have a medium to very high deductible amount that the insured pays before insurance company co-payments start. A typical policy may have a $1000 deductible, pay 80% of the next $5000 and 100% of remaining covered expenses up to a lifetime maximum of a million dollars or more.

The devil is in the details. Better companies offer policies written in plain language. Benefits and provision are clearly explained and easy to understand. Ask for a sample policy before buying coverage and if the language is arcane, stilted or difficult to understand, look to another company.

Long Term Care Insurance

Since 1950 the over-age-65 population in the U.S. has grown by more than 55%, and the number over age 85 has more than tripled. Our improved longevity has been a blessing, but has increased the probability of nursing home confinement. Insurance to protect family assets against cost of that confinement is something families should consider.

The National Association of Insurance Commissioners offers a Long Term Care

Shopper's guide to help families determine if such coverage is appropriate, and if so, to help them find the right policy. According to the NAIC, a good Long Term Care policy should:

Provide an outline that clearly describes coverage, limitations and exclusions to help consumers compare policies.

Give buyer absolute right to return any policy for a full refund within thirty days of purchase.

Cover Alzheimer's Disease.

Guarantee that the insurance company will renew and cannot cancel the policy. Provide at least one year of nursing home or home health care, including intermediate and custodial care.

A policy should not:

Require insured to be hospitalized before being eligible for benefits. Require insured to receive skilled nursing home care before receiving intermediate or custodial care.

Require nursing home care before it will pay for home health care.

Disability Income Insurance

For most wage earners, loss of earnings would mean immediate hardship and disruption of long-range financial plans. Almost everyone insures property, yet many fail to insure income against loss due to disability. Disability is far more likely than home destruction and the potential loss many times greater. Income protection insurance is available, and relatively inexpensive, but reluctance of buyers and sellers to venture into unfamiliar territory often prevents purchase of this important coverage. Because Disability Income Insurance is less familiar, the coverage so important and so often overlooked by insurance buyers and agents we need go into a little more detail.

These Questions and Answers should be helpful:

Q How much income should be insured.
A Take 70% of gross income, subtract Social Security and employer group benefits.

Buy Disability Income Insurance for the remainder.
Q If disabled, how long must I wait before collecting benefits?
A Waiting periods usually range from 30 to 365 days. You select an "Elimination Period" on the policy application. Premiums are less for Longer Elimination Periods.

Q How long will benefits be paid.
A Benefit Periods generally are from two years to life. Premiums are higher for longer benefit periods.

Q Can I collect benefits if disabled but still able to do some work?
A Depends on your policy's "Definition of Disability." That definition must be met before the insurer pays benefits. Strict definitions require inability to do any gainful work. More liberal definitions pay benefits if the insured is unable to work full time at their regular occupation.

Q Can the company cancel, change or refuse to renew a disability income policy?
A No. If policy is Non Cancellable and Guaranteed Renewable. Otherwise, maybe.

Agents & Brokers

Agents represent a company or companies. Brokers represent buyers. For most buyers it makes little difference which you choose. What is important is to deal with one that is knowledgeable and will help you make good decisions. Like picking a financial planner, finding the right agent or broker should be the start of a long-term relationship. Find one you are comfortable with. Counsel of a professional is advisable when buying insurance. Determining amounts, evaluating contract provisions and selecting the right policy or company can be difficult and time consuming. Working with an experienced agent or broker can take some of the work and risk out of finding the right insurance solutions. Agents or brokers can be helpful in finding the right policy with the right company. An insurance company spreads the risks over large numbers and wide geographical areas and uses premiums to build a pool of money from which it pays claims and administrative expenses. I nsurers must use good judgement in assessing risks and evaluating claims. Additionally, the insurance company must manage the money it collects in premiums. If it fails in any one of these important areas it is likely to become insolvent and unable to pay claims.

The insurance company, like the individual, must manage risks it assumes. Typically, insurance companies reinsure against very large losses, buying coverage from *reinsurance companies* or participating in reinsurance pools through reciprocal agreements. For example, a company insuring homes in Florida is prudent to reinsure against catastrophic claims due to hurricanes.

The insurance company, like the individual must manage risks and assets. The insurance buyer should select companies with reputations for good management and fairness. There are agencies which rate insurance companies, and consumers are wise to review ratings before selecting an insurer.

A Some policies can be changed after issue. A policy that is Non-cancellable and Guaranteed Renewable must be renewed and cannot be cancelled or changed so long as premiums are paid.

Q What about Social Security Payments?

A Potential Social Security disability income benefits reduce the amount of personal coverage you can buy. However, Social Security benefit requirements are very strict and it is usually wise to choose a plan that pays a substitute for Social Security if you collect from your policy but are not eligible for SSI.

With insurance, the Devil, or God, they've said it both ways, they say, is in the details. Read contracts carefully, and/or get advice from a trusted professional. Managing risk and insurance policies is not beyond the ability of readers, however, it is likely more cost effective to turn the matter over to a pro than to spend the time necessary to learn all that may be needed to make sound decisions.

Insurance professionals have the advantage of specialized education and, just as important, experience. Experience with policies and companies that may prove invaluable in risk management decisions. Ultimately, one of the most important risk management decisions for the individual or company may be, *whom should I trust?*

5

Buying a Car

✦

How John & Mary Saved $94,419—
On a Ford

o o o o o o o o o o o o o o o o o o o o o o o o o o o o o o o o o o

There comes a time in the affairs of men when you must take the bull by the tail and face the situation.

—*W. C. Fields*

Summary

*Buying a car, any car, is gonna put a dent in your pocketbook. The newer and **pricier** the car, the bigger the dent. New cars can be tempting and oh so hard to resist, but resistance to car fever may build more than character. John & Mary saved $94,419 when they bought a Ford Taurus. Don't believe it? Well…here's the tale.*

Buying a car is both an emotional and a financial decision. Sexy new models can be expensive and hard to resist. Even though new cars cost more, many find the pleasure of their use worth the price. There is no way to place a value on the enjoyment of a fine machine using state-of-the-art technology to achieve new standards of performance and convenience. Owning and operating such a vehicle titillates the senses. Only the individual can decide if the ride is worth the price. However, it is worthwhile to know what we will pay for the dance before we join the party.

Buying an automobile, any automobile, is costly. The newer and pricier the car, the more the buyer will lose on the deal. I know—one manufacturer of high-end autos touts their vehicles as investments, claiming they retain 80% of value over two years versus 60% for lower priced competitors. Seems to me 20% depreciation on $80,000 comes to $16,000, whereas 40% of $30,000 is $12,000, you tell me. If your investment advisor recommends a deal that cannot make a profit and in a good year will lose sixteen grand, you might want to shop for a new advisor. If we pay a little less for the ride, what difference does it make? Well, as mentioned before, with a little finagling, John and Mary saved $94, 419. Here's how it happened.

John and Mary were concerned about their automobile's reliability. Only two gears worked. Reverse and Park. The engine burned equal parts gas and oil, one window rolled down but not up, another rolled up but not down. The left front fender was dented so the tire screeched on big bumps. The right headlight was held in place with duct tape and the left rear door was fastened with a bungee strap. John and Mary decided it was time for a new car. Being realists, they didn't expect much trade in.

They went shopping and liked a new, blue Taurus with all the buttons—and gears. When the dealing was done the price was $18,500. The dealer wouldn't give them anything for their old car, but did offer to haul it as leakage from the differential was eating a hole in his parking lot. They thought the dealer's offer fair but decided to sleep on it. That night, during TV commercials, after reading read War and Peace, John was looking through the classifieds. He found a two-year-old blue Taurus offered for $9,500. They looked at the car, liked it, and the seller accepted their offer of $8,025.

Monthly payments on the used Taurus were $250 for three years. John and Mary had been prepared to pay $377 a month for five years on the new one.

They decided to commit the difference to a Roth IRA. An account was opened to accept the initial $127 monthly difference. Deposits were split among the growth funds and after thirty-six months payments were raised to $377 and continued for two more years. After five years they discontinued payments and forgot about it until they were ready to retire twenty years later. Earnings on the account averaged 9% and the account value grew to $94,419. Who can tell a two-year-old Taurus from a four-year-old Taurus anyway? Still want a new one. Get on the net and find dealer cost for the car you want.

You may want to offer a *local* dealer that cost amount plus a premium, say $500. You should also know, the dealer also gets a *hold back*. A hold back is a percentage of each car invoice price that is paid to dealer based on sales volume. If a dealer sells you a car at his invoice, his net on the deal will be the amount of his hold back.

I personally believe it's better to pay a little more and buy from a local dealer. Cars are pretty good these days but they still break and you'll get better service with a friendlier smile if you bought it where they fix it.

6

Power of Attorney

✦

Agents-Personal Representatives

○ ○

How quaint the ways of Paradox!
At common sense she gaily mocks.

—*W. S Gilbert*

Summary

Power of Attorney or Agency empowers the Agent or Attorney to act for the individual granting the "Power." Agents and personal attorneys usually hold limited power of attorney from individuals they represent. There are times when one is indisposed, out of town on a trip or for a number of other reasons unable to take care of business. It is prudent to grant a trusted person the authority to act when you're laid up, down, or out of town.

Power-of-Attorney or Agency empowers one person to act on behalf of another. The person granting the power or agency is generally referred to as the principal or grantor.

Most think of "Power of Attorney" as an instrument for the elderly rich. While such citizens may be the most frequent users of this useful device, it can be a handy tool for many who do not fit either category because having someone to take care of business when they cannot, or prefer not to, is a good idea for anyone.

When one is sick or disabled, taking care of their business can be troublous enough to cause squabbles in even the most harmonious families. Simple matters like paying routine bills can place families or friends in untenable situations. It is an act of wisdom to head off trouble by authorizing some to act for you if you're laid up, laid down or just out of town. Or, a Power may also be handy when one prefers to distance themselves from a situation, or merely be free of important, but time consuming minutia.

Before setting up a power, consider the following. Do you have special problems to be addressed? What are the rules of institutions you do business with? Some banks, for example, are reluctant to honor a power when it *is not on their form.* Do you do business or hold property in more than one state? My reference lists special rules for most states, so a separate document may be needed for some jurisdictions.

There are different Power-of-Attorney types. For example: A **Durable** Power-of-Attorney persists after a grantor becomes incompetent. A **Springing** Power-of-Attorney is effective only after a disability begins. Section 501 of the Uniform Probate Code authorizes a **Springing-Durable**-Power-of-Attorney. When a Springing or Durable Power is established, how disability or incompetence is determined should be spelled out. A frequently used provision allows for certification by one's personal physician.

The process of granting power of attorney is usually simple and inexpensive, but it is a good idea to have your attorney draw it up. An attorney is trained to help make sure it has special provisions you may need and that your power complies with regulations in areas where you do business. A power of attorney does not take place of a will, but wills and estate plans should include such a provision.

7

When Promises are Broken

o o o o o o o o o o o o o o o o o o o o o o o o o o o o o o o o o

Occam's Razor: As defined in Merriam Webster's Collegiate Dictionary. A scientific and philosophical rule that entities should *not be multiplied unnecessarily which is interpreted as requiring that the simplest of competing theories be preferred to the more complex or that explanations of unknown phenomena be explored first in terms of known quantities.*

Or we could say Keep it Simple.

KISS—*Keep It Simple Savant* and reduce chance of errors and/or misunderstandings.

Summary

When things go wrong, and they will sometime somewhere, your objective is to set them right. In setting things right: Be firm, be persistent, be polite. Courtesy and civility not only reflect good breeding, they are also effective in getting things done. Decide what you want and what you can accept. We must deal with people and situations as they are, not as we wish they were. So, stay cool, avoid emotional reactions and focus on getting the desired result.

When things go wrong and life gets contentious the natural human response is anger. The blame game usually follows. Too often in the anger and blame game we overlook that the important thing is, *to resolve the problem.* To solve the problem somebody's gotta stay cool, and those who keep their cool are more likely to come out on top. So, keep a lid on emotions and concentrate on getting the outcome you want.

Contracts are only as good as those making them and, *the best-laid schemes o' mice and men gang aft agley…* Good insurance agents or companies screw up.

Even the honest, well intentioned salespersons make mistakes. Automobiles sometimes do strange things that are *normal for that model* or within *company* specifications, but not yours. You're looking at a clearly written contract and someone says that's not what we meant. A contractor tells you, we've never had that *problem before! The Supply place assures everyone, it's not our material, the installation was done wrong.*

It may be that you've been done wrong deliberately by an individual or company wanting to make an extra buck cutting corners, or your loss may be the result of honest error. Either way, you want results, not revenge. Revenge may be sweet, but as Confucius said, *"Revenge is the Luxury of fools."* A good result is more practical and the sweetness longer lasting, so if you want to come out whole as quickly and easily as possible, keep your cool, ever *polite, patient and persistent.* As a rule companies, especially large companies, are eager to resolve customer problems or complaints. They are usually amenable to any reasonable offer. However, problems are solved by humans with budgets and when they see up front you're going to hang in there, they are more eager to let you have your way than if they believe you'll just blow up and go away. On the other hand if you abuse the company human up front th ey may be inclined to take the hard line just cause they're piqued off.

Company representatives are generally more experienced in resolving complaints than customers and it is better to have the company human on your side. *You'll catch more flies with a spoonful of honey than a barrel full of vinegar.* Avoid accusations and harsh or inflammatory rhetoric. The company contact must frequently deal with the unreasonable and the irate, so a calm, reasoned approach may be so unusual as to be charming, and it for sure has a better chance of getting them to take your part.

Every dispute will be unique, but the following can be helpful in keeping negotiations on the resolution track. Determine to be: Courteous-Respectful-Thoughtful-Persistent. Before the first problem resolution encounter with the offending party, outline the problem and be ready to suggest a solution. Your outline might include the following:

1.   Outline of problem.

2. Specific points of conflict.

3. How can these points be resolved?

4. What is your very best outcome?

5. What is the least you can settle for?

6. Ask for more than you want.

7. Be prepared to negotiate, reluctantly.

8. Do you need technical help?

9. Do you have a friend or family who can provide technical expertise, or does amount involved make it worth paying for help?

Sic 'em tiger, but start with a SMILE. Ask for advantageous settlement in compensation for your trouble in getting your due. If you must negotiate because it is less trouble to settle than press your claim, be firm and slow to retreat. If you must get tough, losing the smile you started with makes a point. If you don't get results negotiating with local folk, write a letter to the company President or General Manager and send a copy to highest-ranking individual with whom you have discussed your complaint. Don't threaten; just state your case. Brevity is not only the soul of wit, it also has impact. If after a reasonable time the letter does not get results, the next step, should you care to take it, may be to file a complaint with the Better Business Bureau or other appropriate agency. If you take this step, put your complaint in letter form and include copies of prior correspondence. Send copies to representative of offending party.

Next step, should it be necessary and the game is still worth the candle, is to contact an attorney or ombudsman. Furnish your representative copies of prior correspondence and ask what she will charge to correspond with the offending party.

Throughout the complaint process keep in mind your primary objective is to resolve the dispute by getting a result you can accept. Make a settlement offer part of every written or verbal communication. Volumes have been written on this subject, but the bottom line is, stay focused on the outcome you want and avoid emotional reactions. Emotional reactions tend to complicate matters; however, although showing you're really hacked at the right time in the right way can sometimes be constructive.

8

Your Financial Plan

o o o o o o o o o o o o o o o o o o o o o o o o o o o o o o o o o o o o o
The longest journey begins with a single step. Chinese Proverb

Summary

For many, the most difficult part of financial planning seems to be getting started. It is a chore, but it is an important chore. A good financial plan will educate and motivate. And, there can be no doubt that motivation has a major role in a successful financial plan. A good financial plan tells where you are and helps define where you want to go. It also maps out the path to your goals and points out ways to avoid hazards that might wreck your plans. A good financial plan is likely to double the rate at which you accumulate wealth.

Should you get professional help? Probably, but do your homework first. The more you know, the better prepared you will be to work with a financial planning professional.

Well begun is half done, so let us begin:

1. Present situation. Review income, expenses, savings and investments.

2. Define objectives. Set priorities and timelines. Be specific and realistic. Retirement income of $4500 monthly might be a retirement income goal.

3. Develop a plan to meet objectives. Retirement income of $4500 is a goal. Pension and Social Security are expected to be $3500. Develop a plan to make up the remaining $1000.

4. Implement Plan. You now know where you are and where you want to go.

Just do it. Well begun is half done.

Financial Planning Worksheet

Name_____

Date Birth_____Occupation_____

Name_____

Date Birth_____Occupation_____

Children: Names & Date of Birth

_____

Personal Objectives and Priorities—1 Highest

Comments_____

_____

Please assign priority to these financial planning functions:

____Savings/Investment

____Estate Planning

____Life Insurance

____College Savings

____Retirement Income

____Budgeting

____Disability Income

_____Other

_____Other

_____Other

Please rank the following financial objectives:

____Reduce Income Tax

____Build Education Fund

____Provide for Death of Wage Earner

____Provide for Disability of Wage Earner

_____Other

_____Other

_____Other

Please rank the following Investment priorities.
_____Safety
_____Growth
_____Liquidity
_____Current Income
_____Future Income
_____Other
_____Other

Over next twenty years what rate of inflation do you expect?
0 1 2 3 4 5 6 7 8 9 10

_____

Over next twenty years do you expect income to: Increase/Decrease?
By what percentage?_____

Net Worth

Assets

Savings Accounts_____
Checking Accounts_____
Cert. Deposit_____
Life Ins. Cash Value_____
Investments_____ _____
Residence_____ _____
Real Estate (ex. Res.)_____ _____
Business Interests_____ _____
Retirement Plans_____ _____
Other_____
Other_____
Other_____

Liabilities

Home Mortgage_____
Credit Cards_____
Business Debts_____
Tax Liabilities_____
Other_____

Other_____

Other_____

Other_____

Total: Assets_____ Liabilities_____

Net Worth: Assets minus Liabilities_____

Comments_____

_____Good Luck!

Section Two
Investments

o o o o o o o o o o o o o o o o o o o o o o o o o o o o o o o o o o o o o o o o

There are two times in life we should not speculate,
when we cannot afford it
and when we can.

—Mark Twain

9

Investing: The Big Picture

o o o o o o o o o o o o o o o o o o o o o o o o o o o o o o o o o o

Predictions are hard, especially about the future.

—Neils Bohrs, Nobel Prize Winner, Physics 1922

Summary

I nvesting is often confused with speculating. Investing is the practice of managing an investment portfolio for long term results. Speculating is trading for quick profits. Investing, it's hard to lose money; speculating, it's hard not to.

Invest for long-term results and, in what makes you comfortable. Commitment is very important to successful investing. Few remain committed if they are not comfortable. Find your comfort zone, get committed and then diversify, diversify, diversify. Spread investments across economic sectors, international borders and among growth stock, value stock and bonds. Ignore short-term results and predictions. Careful-Thoughtful-Prudent are watchwords for serious investment until the nest egg is sufficient to guarantee financial security. Be open minded about advice or investment opportunities, but remain skeptical. Your own good judgement is the best protection against error or malfeasance of others. Beware, be aware, be informed.

"It was the best of times, it was the worst of times." It would seem Charles Dickens might have been writing about America in the twenty-first century rather than England of the nineteenth. Current headlines paint dim views of our economy and the World seems always poised on the brink of chaos or great prosperity. Legitimate concerns or baseless fears mingle with optimism and *irrational exuberance* to feed our uncertainties. Those uncertainties drive market volatility. Understandably, investors fear to venture into troubled waters, but the waters are always troubled—whether we know it or not. The time to invest is almost always *now*. With that in mind let's take a look at opposing views of recent history.

On the down side, business seems to be faltering under the weight of recent heavy events. Corporate layoffs make daily headlines as industry giants around the globe downsize to cope with reduced demands for products and services. Small business, the big driver in the new economic dynamic takes one hit after another. Legislative responses to real and perceived problems give rise to fear more than hope.

War on Drugs. Nine-one-one. The war on terrorism. Iraq I. Iraq II. Social, religious and economic unrest. *War and rumors of war.*

Drugs, and our star-crossed efforts to control their use and abuse seem to threaten the very foundations of our society. They corrupt our young, damage our institutions. Huge profits from dealin' corrupt legitimate enterprise. We seem to have forgotten the lesson of Prohibition and build more prison walls. We interdict and incarcerate, but the problem compounds and solutions escape us.

A poorly designed and badly managed welfare program destroys families, perpetuates poverty and nurtures a culture with little regard for property or authority. Generation after generation sift down through our *social safety nets.* Discouraged and disillusioned by experience, too many fail to find their place in the Dreamscape painted by those selling the dreams.

Shortsighted profiteering lays waste to the planet and timorous efforts to deal with the problems are more than offset by emerging nations aspiring to the commercial mainstream, or merely trying to feed their starving. For the hungry, or the greedy, environmental concerns remain a distant priority. Yet, unless current destructive trends are reversed, humanity will drown in its own filth.

On the other hand...

Our nation and the World have enjoyed more than half a century of relative peace and prosperity. Productivity has increased at an unprecedented pace. Innovations in technology continue to create new devices and facilitate exchange of information making the world's rapidly increasing store of knowledge ever more accessible, and valuable.

Easier information exchange increases research effectiveness and helps to create better ways to get things done. Each new discovery leads to others in a dynamic upward spiral that improves our living standards and creates new sources of wealth and opportunity.

The economies of nations become daily more interrelated and interdependent, creating commonality of interests that force cooperation. Communism is a failed experiment, and the World moves ever closer to a system of international free trade that makes the flow of goods, services and information increasingly efficient. Through education, science and industry we are finding solutions to our problems, and in those solutions we are finding answers to questions we didn't even know to ask. Also in those questions and answers is wealth and prosperity previous generations could not have imagined.

Even though both viewpoints reach a bit, each has a measure of veracity. Similar paragraphs could be written about any period in history. So if we wait for smooth waters, we could be waiting and waiting and…

Uncertainty is with us always, but today's instant communication in rhetoric of daily doom exaggerates ordinary cycles. In the short run financial markets are driven to extremes, but over the long haul they must reflect real values. Real values should continue to grow, but *predictions are difficult.*

Market response to any stimulus, good or bad, is almost always far out of proportion to the event's real significance. And, the over reaction is greater when the news is bad. So, when the markets move dramatically down in response to bad news, there is often opportunity.

That may not be much to hang your money on, but with all due respect to market mavens who quote sophisticated technical analysis and in hallowed tones confidently predict market moves over the next few hours, days or weeks, it's about as good as it gets. Those gals and guys predicting make good cases for their opinions and they are fun to watch, but their guesses are no better than yours or mine.

To support that statement, I offer the Wall Street Journal's Darts vs Pros competition. Each quarter top investment analysts pit their picks against a portfolio chosen by throwing darts at a Wall Street Journal stock listing. The counting period is one calendar quarter. There have been dramatic wins and losses on both sides, but in the contest's long history, performance difference between Darts and Pros has been insignificant.

Keep in mind Dart's vs. Pros deals with short-term results. Over the long haul, performance predictions based on careful review of relevant data have validity and are worthy of consideration.

It has been my experience that *investing* is often confused with speculating. *Investing is the practice of managing a portfolio for long term results. Speculating is trading for quick profits.* Investing, it's hard to lose money; speculating, it's hard not to.

Roughly 90% of speculators[1] lose money. It's probably mere coincidence that those playing casino games meet with about the same rate of success. Don't misunderstand me. Either game is fun, just don't play with your serious money. For most, successful investing is picking a diversified portfolio of mutual funds and devoting your energies to making money in ways you enjoy or are trained for. It's a good bet a physician or plumber will make more doctoring or plumbing than trading stocks. For either, playing the stock market may be a fun hobby, but if they're gonna make it their living they will need to beat others who make it their living.

If you buy and sell stock carefully, always with an eye to the long term, you are likely to make more than in a mutual fund portfolio. You would also avoid mutual fund management fees. However, managing an investment portfolio is hard, demanding work. Most investors will do better devoting their energy to what they know best and paying a pro to manage their investments.

Most investors should concentrate on diversifying among economic sectors, geographical areas, and types of stock. Spread it around, splitting between growth and value stock and leaven with bonds. Spreading it around reduces risk and increases stability. Properly done, prudent, thoughtful diversification gets desirable results with a relatively small impact on yield.

◆   ◆   ◆

Harry Markowitz, Merton Miller and William Sharpe earned a Nobel Prize in Economic Science for their work on this matter. The Nobel Laureates defined performance contrasts among investment categories by calculating historical

---

1.   Ibbotson & Associates

yields and developing return indexes for a wide variety of investment combinations. Markowitz, Miller and Sharpe demonstrated that stocks and bonds usually do not experience best performance under the same circumstances and that frequently, a market impetus, which causes one to gain value, will cause the other to lose. Their data also revealed that although common stock investments were risky and unpredictable in the short term, risk diminished and return became more predictable over time.

◆   ◆   ◆

Early on when developing an investment plan, find your comfort zone. With your advisor, *talk of shoes and ships and sealing wax* and many investment things. Decide where you can put your hard-earned bucks and still sleep well. If you aren't sleeping well with your investments, it will be hard to remain committed, especially when times get tough.

Commitment is more important than what we invest in, it can keep us on track when times get tough. And, times will get tough. Markets will go up and down. There will be months or years of gloom and doom and months or years of up, up, up. Those who can stay the roller coaster course will win. They will win because in investing, like anything else, persistence and commitment pay dividends.

Once you have developed your investment philosophy, keep focus ever on the long haul. The objective for serious money is to provide lifetime financial security. The market will go up and down, there will be wild swings, and precipitous drops may be followed by explosive growth. There will extended periods of go-go and seemingly endless months or years of no-go. The wise investor rides with both, always taking the long view. Short-term predictions are silly, usually meaningless and often costly to those who march to their piper's swinging beat.

I like a quote from Jack Bogle of Vanguard Funds, *I have said many times that explanations of daily moves of the market are tales told by idiots, full of sound and fury signifying nothing. It's entertainment, people speaking with a high degree of assurance about things in which there can be no level of assurance…anyone who pays attention to them is just plain crazy.*

The pretty people on television are entertaining, but don't let them distract you from your bottom line on the investment big picture. Diversify, look to the long term and ignore the daily drivel.

10

Stocks, Bonds, Mutual Funds REITs & DRIPs

○ ○

The Chinese symbol for crisis combines signs for opportunity and danger.

Summary

Stock and Bond holdings are usually the bed rock of long term investment portfolios. Common Stock represents ownership. Bonds represent interest-bearing loans to a company or government. Mutual Funds are pools of investment money under control of a manager that makes investment decisions. DRIPs—a program where investors by stock direct from companies. REITs are mutual funds that invest in real estate.

Over long periods, common stock has substantially outperformed other generally available investments. In the short run, stock investments tend to be risky and returns unpredictable. Over time; however, risk diminishes, and returns become more predictable. This condition strongly suggests that buying stocks and bonds with a long-term perspective is prudent and wise, and that buying stocks and bonds for the short run is speculative and, perhaps even foolish. Stock and Bond traders make markets in stocks and bonds by matching buyers and sellers. Prices fluctuate as interest in buying or selling shares wax and wane. Stock prices are published daily in most major newspapers, on television and on the Internet.

For the vast majority, Stocks and Bonds will be an investment portfolio's bed-rock. Whether one invests direct or through Mutual Funds, they should have a basic knowledge of Stocks and Bonds. *Common Stock represents equity or owner-ship. Bonds represent loans.*

Common Stock owners participate in management and company profits. Common stock owners participate in management decisions and if the company is dissolved Common Stock owners will share assets and surplus.

Preferred Stock, like bonds, represents debt—interest bearing obligations. Preferred stock owners have preference in distribution of profits and assets. Preferred stock-holders[1] are paid first. Preferred shareholders have no say in management of the company. Preferred Stock values are fixed and do not fluctuate with business profit or loss. So though Preferred Stock cannot lose value, neither can it gain except for fluctuations caused by the value of its earnings.

A Company's Preferred Stock often has a call price. When a call price is listed, the issuing company has retained the right to redeem the shares at any time by paying the call price. Preferred Stock owners may have the right to exchange Preferred Stock for Common Stock.

Bonds, like preferred stock, represent debt obligations of a company or government.

Bonds also are issued at a fixed rate of interest for a fixed period of time. Preferred Stock and Bond values fluctuate with interest rates. When market interest rates go up, Preferred Stock or Bond values go down and when market interest rates go down, Preferred Stock and Bond values will rise.

This market value fluctuation occurs because the principal sum required to earn a given amount changes. For example:

A $1000 Bond paying 5% earns $50 per year. If the market interest rate remains at 5% the Bond or Preferred Stock value remains at $1000. If the market interest rate decreases to 4% the bond value rises as principal required to earn $50 will increase to $1250. If Market Interest rates should increase to 6% the principal required to earn $50 would drop to $834.

Market values of Bonds or Preferred Stock adjust to these changes. Common Stock earns dividends when the company makes a profit. The price of Common

---

1.   Terms stockholder and shareholder are used interchangeably.

Stock changes with conditions that influence the company's ability to produce profits, and with investors' expectation for the company's future. Current profits and investor expectation determine prices investors are willing to pay for shares.

A company may not be making money today, but if investors believe they will do so in the future, they may speculate on those future profits and buy shares of a company that is currently unprofitable. The day-to-day price investors pay for a company's stock may have no relation to its real value and is often determined by investor moods.

Much is made over the greater fool theory, *I know I'm a fool to pay so much for this stock but somewhere there will be a bigger fool who will pay me more.* It is best to neither fool be, and stick to decisions based on actual value. Over the long term the value of a company's stock will be determined by its ability to provide goods or services at a profit.

If a company has no earnings there will be no dividends, and if a company has no earnings the value of the stock is likely to decrease. If a company is making money and has good prospects, its stock is likely to rise.

So, the value of a company's stock is influenced by current profit or loss and, investor expectations for the future. When earnings are expected to increase share values go up and conversely negative expectations depress share values.

In the short run, expectations are often the greater influence, in the long run, company performance is the dominant factor. Over the long term a company must be able to deliver goods or services at competitive prices and make a profit; if it does not, the price of its shares will decrease. If a company remains unprofitable over a long period of time, the company may cease to exist, unless of course, it is subsidized by taxpayers or other dupes.

Short term Common Stock prices change dramatically and irrationally, what is sometimes referred to a random walk or meander. Investor expectations may be based in reality or in nonsense, *irrational exuberance* or unreasonably negative expectations. If we consistently make good guesses we may profit from short-term volatility, but history tells us we'd be a fool to bet our nest egg money on our guesses.

Mutual Funds

Mutual Funds[2] are a method of reducing investment risk by diversifying, or spreading it around. The strategy probably dates back into pre-history but the earliest example I found is with Phoenician traders.

Huge price differentials among ports of call offered enormous profit potential but, sailing costly ships loaded with valuable goods across great oceans meant trusting captains to brave storms, elude pirates and not steal the ship. Risky business.

There were fortunes to be made, but one of every five ships was lost, a ruinous disaster for one person owning one ship. Pooling resources allowed several ship owners to share risk and rewards. A Mutual Fund?

Mutual Funds are jointly owned investment companies. The fund manager is bound by the mutual fund's *Investment guidelines* as defined in the *Fund Prospectus*.

Managers may have complete discretion in buying and selling investments, or be limited to a specific objective or investment guidelines. A fund's guideline may restrict investments to corporate stocks and bonds, real estate, currencies, to geographical areas, business sectors or company size. Management costs are paid out of fund assets. The major advantage of mutual funds is diversification and relief from management decisions. The primary disadvantage is that investment returns are reduced by costs of managing the funds.

For investors who do not want to devote substantial time and energy to managing investments, mutual funds are often a good choice because they allow even very small investment to be spread around, and reduce need for research and tough buy-sell decisions.

Today, thousands of mutual funds are available. The broad range of general and specialized funds permits investors to choose investment strategies suited to their individual objectives and temperaments. The number and variety of fund types also makes diversification easy. Small regular investments, say from payroll deduction, allow investments to be spread over different countries, companies

---

2.   Microsoft Encarta multimedia encyclopedia offers one of the better and more detailed explanations of Mutual Funds.

and economic sectors. A few dollars automatically transferred from a checking account can go into both conservative and aggressive stock and/or be split among many companies.

Mutual funds allow a little money to be in a lot of places. Most mutual funds are classed as open-end funds, meaning that the fund will redeem shares on request. Thus, the number of shares of an open-end mutual fund is not fixed, but fluctuates as new shares are bought and sold to investors. The offering price and redemption price of open-end funds are based on the total market value of securities it owns.

Sales commissions, or *loads,* may be included in the share price. *Front Load* funds charge commissions at time of purchase. *Back Load,* deducts commissions when money is withdrawn. *No Load* funds do not charge commissions. All funds have sales costs and management expenses which must be recouped, so there are charges extant in any mutual fund purchase. Charges vary widely between funds and must be stated in the prospectus.

Closed-end funds generally have a fixed number of shares that are traded on stock exchanges. Shares are bought and sold at market price plus commission. Shares of closed-end funds may sell at prices that are above or below asset value.

The principal advantage of mutual funds is they allow a lot of diversification with even small amounts of money and relief from management decisions. The primary disadvantage is returns are reduced by costs of managing the money pool and the fund's investment portfolio. The diversification that protects investors against business risk also reduces their chances for making big profits off big winners. Mutual funds reduce the chance you will either get killed, or make a killing.

DRIPs

DRIPs are direct investment plans. Participating companies sell stock to the public without services of a broker. The advantage of DRIPs is there are no fees or commissions. DRIPs' disadvantage is fewer stocks are offered so diversification potential is limited compared to mutual funds, and there are no brokers to advise. A DRIP may have purchase agreements with any number of different companies and each purchase is spread among all companies contracting with the plan. Most DRIPs allow small systematic purchases through salary deduction agreements or automatic bank drafts. Expenses are usually less than with a mutual fund because management is simpler and costs are often shared by companies that sell stock through the DRIP.

REITs

Real Estate Investment Trusts are mutual funds that invest in real estate. Fund earnings may be distributed to investors or reinvested. Investment returns, as with mutual funds or DRIPs, are derived from both earnings and asset appreciation. REITs invest in both broad and narrow real estate markets. Again like mutual funds, investors can select from REITs with different investment objectives.

11

Annuities

○ ○
We promise…read it carefully, read it again slowly and carefully.
Then, read it again very slowly, and very carefully.

Summary

Annuities are insurance company agreements to trade a principal sum for income. Annuity contracts can exchange a lump sum for income or accumulate deposits and earnings over time, then distribute principal and earnings in an income stream. Annuities offer tax advantages during both accumulation and distribution periods. However, tax penalties and insurance company withdrawal charges in early years make annuities unsuitable in the short term. In general, annuities are advantageous only when withdrawals will be made after annuitant attains age 59 1/2, retires or plans to hold the contract ten years or more.

Many readers may be familiar with annuities as insurance contracts that accumulate tax-deferred retirement funds for later pay out. Annuity earnings are not taxed until withdrawn account values grow faster than in equivalent taxable accounts. Taxes on annuity earnings are due when money is withdrawn. A tax penalty1 of 10% is imposed on annuity withdrawals made before the annuitant is age 59 ¡. Taxes and penalties discourage use of annuities for short-term investments. There are exceptions, so if you need money from an annuity during the penalty period, check to see if you qualify for one of those exceptions.

Annuities are flexible financial instruments offering a wide variety of accumulation and distribution arrangements. They can be valuable tools for managing income streams for retirees and beneficiaries. Beyond these basics, annuities drop into an abyss of confusing federal regs and arcane jargon where we need not go. Like any matter involving taxes, government regulation and insurance, annuities can be perplexing.

However, if you really want to go there...

Annuities may be *qualified*[1] or *non-qualified*, fixed or variable, certain, immediate or deferred. An annuity may not even be an annuity! How could anyone be confused? I'll try to make some sense of the muddle but if I become hopelessly confused, just pray for me and skip to another chapter.

Annuities are purchased through or underwritten by insurance companies. They are designed as retirement accounts and permit interest or investment earnings to accumulate tax-deferred. Annuity earnings are taxed when they are withdrawn.

While annuities are most often used to create an income stream for the owner or depositor, they are also useful for providing income to other beneficiaries. Life insurance policies often pay benefits as an annuity income. So do lotteries. Rather than getting into annuity complexities, let's look at how they work for typical investors by comparing a Certificate of Deposit to an interest bearing annuity.

A $100,000 deposit in a 20-year CD is compared to a $100,000 payment into an annuity. Both earn 6%. Our investor has a combined federal and state marginal tax rate of 33% (tax rate on last dollar earned).

At the end of the twenty years CDs have grown to $219,112. The Annuity is worth $320,713. The CD is worth less because each year 1/3 of earnings (33%) were paid out in taxes.

When the accounts are converted to income, still earning at 6%, the annuity has annual earnings of $19,243 versus $12,896 for the CD.

The disadvantage of the annuity is that it cannot be government insured. The safety of an annuity depends on the strength of the insurance company making the guarantees. Certificates of Deposit, on the other hand, are guaranteed by the Federal Deposit Insurance Corporation. Most insurance agents suggest it is prudent to stick with highly regarded companies. Companies rated A (Excellent) or

---

1.   *Qualified* means contributions are tax deductible. *Non-qualified* deposits are made from after-tax earnings.

better by Best's Review. Best's is deemed to be the gold standard for insurance company ratings.

Deferred Annuities

Deferred Annuities accumulate earnings over a period of time then offer the *annuitant* pay-out options. Typical pay-out choices are, five, ten, twenty years, or joint and survivor. Joint and survivor option continues income for life of the *annuitant* and named *joint annuitant*. Pay-out choices may be for: A specified period of time, referred to as, *Period Certain*, say five or ten years. Or pay-out may be continued for life of annuitant, or for joint lifetimes of annuitant and a dependent.

The longer the pay-out period the lower the pay-out income. For example:

If life income for a 65-year-old male were $1,000, joint and survivor life income for a 65-year-old male and a 65-year-old female would be about $880 per month.

Immediate Annuities

Immediate annuities use a lump sum to purchase an income stream that will begin on a stated date. Immediate annuities offer the same pay-out options as deferred annuities.

Variable Annuities

Variable annuities have the same properties as regular or fixed annuities but offer investment choices that include mutual funds as well as interest bearing accounts.

Variable annuity pay-outs usually fluctuate with experience of the investment accounts. They also offer periodic withdrawal arrangements in amounts specified by the annuity owner. Variable annuities usually offer a guaranteed income option.

Indexed Annuities

Indexed annuities guarantee that returns will match that of a stock index less a discount. A typical indexed annuity might guarantee a yield equaling S&P 500 less 1.5%.

Indexed annuities can be valuable financial tools, but read and understand before you buy. Don't be embarrassed to ask for help. Computing yields and understanding calculation methodology is not rocket science, but I had to go to quantum physicist Richard Koshel to get a grip on one company's product.

Charitable Annuities

Charitable annuities, as the name implies, are used to facilitate charitable gifts. Charitable annuities may be purchased from an insurance company, combined with a trust, or made by direct arrangement with a charitable organization. Charitable annuities can be direct or remainder interest gifts. In remainder interest annuities, as in Remainder Trusts, the donor receives income for life, then at donor's death what is left in the account inures to the charity.

Income tax advantages of Charitable Annuities can be substantial. Deposits are tax-deductible and there may be credits against both current and future income. A portion of the income from a charitable annuity.

Charitable annuities also are valuable estate planning tools. For example, they can be used to buy life insurance to help pay estate settlement costs. Or, they can eliminate taxes when highly appreciated assets are used to provide income.

◆   ◆   ◆

Should you consider annuities for your savings? Probably, but annuities work only for long term savings. In the short run, advantages are offset by taxes and penalties. Buying an annuity wisely involves some homework and shopping. As with just about anything involving insurance or insurance companies, I recommend using a professional insurance agent. A good agent can help you decide, if an annuity is appropriate, and if so, what money belongs in annuities. They can also do the shopping. Shopping among insurance companies for annuities is a fit pursuit only for professionals, dedicated hobbyists and confirmed masochists.

12

Life Insurance

o o o o o o o o o o o o o o o o o o o o o o o o o o o o o o o o o o

Buy term and invest the difference?

Summary

Perhaps the advice most frequently given about life insurance is "Never mix life insurance and investments." It is also probably the dumbest. It is especially bad advice for professionals, business owners or others likely to accumulate substantial estates. Buy term and invest the difference? If life insurance needed less than ten years, probably. If life insurance needed longer than ten years, probably not. Every life insurance purchase is unique and cookie cutter platitudes should not be used in the purchase decision. Life insurance forms best suited to investment are Variable Universal Life and Single Premium Life.

Life insurance has preferential tax status because providing financial security for dependents is considered a socially desirable act to be encouraged. The following tax incentives encourage life insurance ownership:

Earnings on life insurance cash values are not taxed as income.
Loans against life insurance policy cash values are not taxable.
Life insurance proceeds are not taxed as income.

These tax advantages give life insurance an advantage over other investments. An advantage that is especially meaningful to those in higher tax brackets. Life insurance tax advantages are also meaningful to those likely to accumulate substantial estates. Short and long-term tax considerations should be a part of every life insurance purchase. With that background, let's review the basic life insurance

51

forms. Then, after laying that groundwork, consider life insurance investment possibilities.

Term Life Insurance

Term life: Insured dies—company pays. Term life, as the name implies is for a term, or period of time. At the end of the term, or insured period, you make a new deal. A term policy may be *guaranteed renewable* meaning the company must issue a new policy. The policy may also be *non-cancelable* meaning the *rate*1 cannot be increased and the company cannot refuse to issue a new policy due to a change in insured's health.

Term insurance periods usually range from one to twenty years. One, Five and Ten year policies are most common. Term life insurance costs less because the insurance company is obligated only for the finite period and *payment of insurance proceeds is merely a possibility* that occurs only if insured dies when the insurance is in force. With *Whole Life, Straight Life* or other permanent life insurance plans *payment of proceeds is a certainty* if the policy is in force.

Obviously, as term life insurance builds no cash value, it cannot be an investment. Term life description is included in this chapter merely for reader convenience and to help make comparisons easier.

Whole Life or Straight Life

Whole life, or Straight Life, is so called because premiums remain level for life. If the policy remains in force, the insurance company will pay the policy face amount when the insured dies.

To make sure insurance companies are able to pay, they are required to maintain cash reserves. If a policy is surrendered during the insured's lifetime, the cash *reserved* to guarantee the company's capacity to pay, called *cash value,* reverts to the policyowner. While the policy is in force, the policyowner has the right to borrow against policy cash values. *Policy loans* are made at favorable interest rates and repayment is not required. If the insured dies with *a policy loan outstanding the loan amount is deducted from life insurance proceeds. Policy* loan rates are stated in the policy.

Some policies allow *zero interest2* loans. With a zero interest loan, the company actually charges interest on the amount borrowed, and pays an equal rate on the borrowed money, creating a *wash loan*. The reason for this convoluted handling is to get around regulations requiring loans to bear interest if they are to be treated as loans for tax purposes. A wash loan, or wash anything, is a transaction which results in no gain or loss.

Zero interest loans are offered to make policies more attractive. *A policy allowing cost free access to cash values is more valuable because policy loans are generally not considered income and create no tax liabilities.* Insurance companies can afford to make such loans because most policyowners accumulating substantial cash values in life insurance policies do not borrow against cash values and, are quick to repay loans when they do make them.

Policyowners with large cash reserves in quality policies find it advisable to leave the cash values intact because they create no present or future tax liability. Policy earnings paid as death benefits escape income taxation.

Universal Life

As bad as they say or as good as it sounds?

Every time a philosophy major tells me, *it's neither good nor bad, it just is*, I want to strangle them, but that's Universal Life.

A Ferrari Testerosa is a great car, it can exceed speed limits on most roads by more than a hundred miles per hour, it can really haul ah...er, two people, but it will get stuck on a beach and is no good at all for carrying cotton. So it is with Universal life. Used properly it is a flexible and valuable financial instrument. Improperly applied it will likely disappoint. In the right time and place, Universal life is likely to be substantially superior to other policy forms.

Universal life policies are complex, more so than many who sell or buy them understand. While it is not necessary for consumers and agents to know everything about Universal life, both buyers and sellers should know how they work and have a general idea of when they should or should not be used.

How Universal Life Works

Universal life policies separate cash values and insurance costs. Payments made into Universal life policies are held in an interest-bearing side fund. Premiums are deducted from the side fund to pay for monthly renewable term life insurance. Simple enough.

So long as total of payments and earnings on the side fund are sufficient to pay the life insurance cost, no problem. Everything hunky dory. However, universal life planned premiums are set by agents and policy owners, and planned premiums are based on projections of insurance costs and side fund earnings. Sometimes agents eager to make a sale, or buyers eager to get the lowest possible premium, go with a planned premium based on *irrationally exuberant* projections. If the performance does not meet those optimistic projections the side fund may be depleted. If the side fund collapses the policyowner must increase premiums or reduce benefits, otherwise, the policy will lapse. Insurance companies furnish annual statements of account values, but too often policyowners are too busy to read them. Most folks buy a life insurance policy then put it away and forget about it. With a Universal Life policy, annual statements should be reviewed with interest. Anytime the po licy account value is less than it was the preceding year, there is reason for concern, and possibly need for remedial action.

Should you be the owner of an under performing Universal Life policy, get with your agent. Determine how much additional premium would be needed to bring the policy up to speed. I suggest one projection using current average crediting rates over last ten years and another at two per-cent less than that average. If a UL policy is not meeting expectations and the problem is caught in early years the deficiency can usually be remedied with small changes in premium or benefits. If the policy remains under funded until the insured is at an advanced age the repair will likely be costly and require a substantial increase in premium or reduction in insurance benefits.

The key to universal life is starting with a realistic planned premium and reviewing annual statements.

Variable Universal Life

Nobody understands Quantum Physics—Richard Feynman. Nor, it seems, does anyone understand Variable Universal Life.

Though Variable Universal Life policies are not quantum physics most consumers and agents seem completely baffled by them. VUL policies are complex, but they are merely universal life policies with a variety of investment options. VULs, like regular universal life policies, use side funds, but where conventional universal life has a single interest bearing account, VULs offer other options. Typical VULs offer guaranteed interest accounts, money market funds, REITs and mutual funds of almost every stripe. At best VUL is like a regular Universal Life policy on steroids, at worst it's more like Universal Life anorexia nervosa.

If VUL is complicated, sometimes a bit risky, and agents and consumers fear to tread there, why not just stick to simpler policy forms? Good question and one I've asked myself a few times. VUL should be considered because, also like Universal Life, there are many times when it is appropriate, and when it is appropriate, any other policy form is probably grossly inferior.

Variable Universal life is appropriate whenever the purchaser is comfortable investing in stocks and bonds, there is a long term need for life insurance and the buyer can afford to *overfund* the policy.

So, VUL isn't so complicated after all. "Premiums" are paid into the policy and split among the different accounts as directed by the policyowner. Then, as with regular UL policies monthly term life insurance costs are deducted from account values.

All Variable Universal Life policies have internal charges for costs in addition to deductions for life insurance. These charges vary widely from company to company. So, with the counsel of a financial advisor knowledgeable about VUL and investments, shop and compare.

Single Premium Life

Assassinated by TAMRA! Reborn as Annuity-SPL.
(Chapter 19 offers more detail on Single Premium Life policies.)

So called Single Premium Life policies under new rules work like this. The revived Single Premium Life scheme splits the lump sum deposit between a life insurance policy and a single premium immediate annuity. One-fifth of the deposit goes directly to the policy, the remainder to a single premium immediate annuity. The annuity makes four annual payments to the life insurance policy equal to the annual IRS guideline maximum. Or, if a Single Premium Variable Universal Life, into the policy's investment accounts. Deductions are made to pay for the life insurance. As most of the life insurance face amount is covered by the lump sum premium, there is little actual insurance to buy and costs are low.

The result is a tax-sheltered return that closely matches taxable investments with equivalent risks. SPLs permit "zero" interest loans that do not require repayment and allow no cost access to the tax-sheltered earnings. If policy owner dies with policy loans outstanding, loan amounts are deducted from policy proceeds. If earnings are not taken from the policy they are paid to beneficiaries as a life insurance *death benefit*, which readers will remember is *not taxable as income*.

The only significant difference under the new rules is that, with the Annuity-SPL split, in the first five years the policyowner has income tax liability for annuity earnings. The split also creates a slightly higher insurance cost and a greater death benefit because part of the lump sum is in the annuity rather than the insurance policy.

Life Insurance as an Investment

IRS limits the amount that can be paid into a life insurance policy. The *Guideline Premiums* are determined by the age and health of the insured and the life insurance Face Amount. The guidelines limit both annual and lifetime payments. If the guidelines are violated, the policy is classified *Not Life Insurance* and loses life insurance tax benefits.

The guideline maximums are enough to allow a life insurance policy to be substantially *overfunded*. Overfunding increases the policy side fund and exposure to investment gains. This situation, combined with the varied investment options available with Variable Universal Life policies opens up meaningful possibilities for tax favored returns.

Considering VUL as an investment is a time consuming undertaking, but it may be time well spent. However, go gently and carefully. I suggest consult with CLU and a CPA familiar with VUL policies.

Life insurance proceeds, or death benefits, are included in the policyowner's estate. This will be covered in some detail in the Estate Planning section, but policy ownership should be considered when applying for a life insurance policy.

Is death benefit a misnomer, or perhaps an oxymoron?

Buy Term and Invest the Difference?

Should one buy term and invest the difference? Maybe, maybe not. A typical life insurance policy may require twelve to fourteen years to equal buying term and investing the difference. On the other hand, a high quality Variable Universal Life policy at maximum allowable premium and moderate yields may beat term and investing the difference in as few as four years. There are lots of variables and many unknowns and the term or permanent answer always depends on individual situations. Higher incomes and potential for wealth accumulation can increase likelihood permanent insurance is best choice.

13

Sleep Well

○ ○

The only thing certain in life is change.
Don't lose balance over the unexpected.

Once upon a time a little old woman and a little old man came to the office with a princely sum inherited from her little old mamma and little old poppa. This money, they said, they really don't need, but would put it away for their grandchildren. They did not know me. A family friend had sent them my way.

We shook hands around. A charming couple, educated and wise, all roughness worn smooth on the pathways of life. She neat and spry, with lovely gray hair. He trim and wiry, had a gentlemanly flair. He was touching her gently as he held her chair. She smoothed her skirt as she sat. The mister leaned back and relaxed.

We settled in with coffee and in just a few minutes it seemed we were all good friends. At first they said the money did not really matter but as we talked it became obvious they had definite ideas. Ideas plural, he one, and she another.

He wanted Safety. She wanted Growth, liked Aggressive Growth and International Mutual Funds. He preferred CDs and Treasuries Though they continued to smile there was iron in their wills.

It didn't take long to see this was going to be interesting. I'm not so much a financial advisor as a financial explainer. One who lays out options, pointing out the pros and cons, helping clients discover what's best for them. I learned long ago that when it goes wrong, as sooner or later it surely will, we can stay friends only if they were party to the choices, the informed guesses.

Finally, after thinking I had a handle on what would suit, we made an appointment, same time next week. Next week, they had different ideas, it was apparent they, she actually, had been doing some reading. So, same time next week, and next week and then the next.

Two months went by. *Mary Alice*, I'll call her, began to come in alone, calling in advance to see when I would have a few minutes, seems Frank was more interested in golf and the timber on the back forty than endless discussions about money that didn't matter anyway. I had learned quite a while back that Mary Alice was a retired concert pianist; that this soft spoken septuagenarian had a keen wit, an engaging sense of humor and a supercharged brain.

Then, on a Friday at 7:45 AM my cell phone beep found my daughter and I leisurely breakfasting at Shipleys when we should have already been at kindergarten.

> Mary Alice by now knew my routine and that I seldom scheduled anything for Friday,
> "Could I stop by the office?"
> "Sure," I said, pleased at the prospect, "I'll be there by nine and we'll have coffee."

I dropped daughter off at school and found Mary Alice chatting with Sharon, my assistant. We were by now, despite our short acquaintance, quite comfortable with each other, like old friends.

"What do I need to do to be a broker?" She asked without preamble.

I told her. She ordered the books and passed the exams in quick time.

My office was an old brown brick house that had served as a church parsonage for three-quarters of a century until the church relocated. With only one broker, my assistant and me, there was plenty of room for another office without crowding anyone. Mary Alice started calling her friends, ladies of similar stripe who had made or inherited money. Money that was often loafing when it should be *working money*. They came, they listened, they liked what they heard and invested. She was having fun and on the way to becoming a successful broker. But, the money really didn't matter. She put in a lot more hours than me. Mary Alice even worked on Friday.

The money that didn't matter. Half went into bonds, half into a diversified group of growth mutual funds. Frank. He's still playing golf, working timber on the back forty and justifiably proud of Mary Alice's new career. The moral of this little tale is life is full of surprises. Some of them will really surprise you. And if you think this is a strange tale, wait until you meet Al, the air conditioning guy.

Section Three
Retirement Planning

○ ○

I've been retired longer than I worked.

The difference between and old man and elderly gentleman is money.

14

Retirement—The Big Picture

o o o o o o o o o o o o o o o o o o o o o o o o o o o o o o o o o o o o

It is not so important to be serious, as to be serious about important things.

—*Robert Hutchins*

Summary

Retirement today, especially for the educated, is often merely a career change; or rearranging work so it accommodates personal preferences. Increasing life expectancies, improved health and vitality, along with broader opportunities for older citizens often make post retirement years more productive than pre-retirement years. Additionally, retirement, whatever form retirement takes, may last a long, long time, so prepare to enjoy.

Most retirement plans are too conservatively invested. Retirement accounts are often considered as investments to be held until retirement. In reality, at retirement, withdrawals may begin, but the principle sum usually remains invested over the retiree's remaining lifetime. Retirement account earnings typically exceed withdrawals and the amount passing with owner's estate is usually greater than when retirement began.

Once upon a time retirement was people too old to work laying down their tools and waiting to die. Just a generation or two ago, folks were expected to work forty or so years until they were sixty-five then rocker on the porch while waiting for the hearse. No longer.

I've been retired longer than I worked. The difference between an old man and an elderly gentleman is money. These two quotes from an elderly gentleman reflect an

63

old verity and a new norm. One—Being old with ample funds is far different from being old and poor. Two—Retirement today may last a long, long time.

Since 1950, the over age 65 population has increased by more than half. The number of old, old, defined as those over 85, has tripled. The over 85 group is expected to double again in the next decade. And, for the first time in history centenarians are raising the needle on the significance meter.

We retire younger, then live to be older. And retirement is not what it used to be. Many now retire in their fifties and are likely to live into their late nineties. Retired no longer means snoring in the recliner. Retirement today often means little more than a career change, or the same career rearranged. Today's retirement dynamics suggest reexamination of traditional thinking on retirement planning is in order.

One truth to beg challenge is those nearing retirement age, whether it be forty-five or eighty-five, should shun growth investments and stick to the safety of interest bearing accounts. Such thinking might make sense for one expected to just sit quietly and count their savings for a few years. However, for the healthy sixty-year-old who's always wanted to start her own business, try a new career, or rearrange the career she loves: Who now has time, where-with-all and prospects for decades of good health, there is still a place for growth investments in the portfolio.

Another long treasured assumption is that savings accumulated in a lifetime of working are depleted to support retirement. That treasured assumption is wrong. Most who saved while working continue to do so after retirement, and even those who were unable to put anything away before retirement usually start afterward.

The reality is the vast majority of Americans increase savings during retirement. There may have been a time when, though the stereotype is not consistent with seniors I have known, retirees were quiet and passive, but for today's retirees, retirement typically means turning hobbies, avocations and dreams into new ventures that make money. For many it will be the first time they are making money doing what they like. The best selling author, Stuart Woods said.

The secret of happiness is finding a way to make a living doing what you like.

Many retirees, especially professionals, who are more likely to have made a career doing things they liked, stay in their chosen field. However, these most fortunate folk usually rearrange commitments so that rather than living to the demands of their work, their work is molded to their preferences.

Today's retirement plan, especially for those reading this book, is unlikely to fit any cookie cutter. Every retirement, like every retiree, is unique. We can't deal with every situation, but in spite of W. C. Fields admonition *that, There's not a generalization in the world that's worth a damn, including this one,* we can in the next four chapters deal with some generalities that may be worth a damn to many who plan to *retire* some day.

We'll explore the realities of retirement planning in the here and now. In doing so we will delve into the experience of others, but please bear with me. First, we gotta do some homework, review a few retirement tools.

15

Tax Sheltered Retirement Accounts

✦

IRAs-TSAs-401Ks, ROTHs, ESOPs & Pension Plans

○ ○

Wealth is an inborn attitude of mind…

—Author Unknown.
Maybe some of us just need an attitude adjustment.

Summary

No area of personal finance seems to attract government attention and med-dling like retirement accounts. In pursuit of sometimes-questionable agendas lawmakers are forever tinkering. The recent crash of important companies prompted a rash of reforms intended to protect retirement accounts, espe-cially those heavily invested in employer's stock. Reforms that attempt to smooth bumps and reduce risks for the inept, the unwary or the greedy, also reduce opportunity for the prudent. And, the rules usually fail in their intent. Do not count on regulations to protect you from charlatans or greedy execu-tives. Those types will always find new and more effective ways to cook the books and parboil investors. Your own vigilance is your best protection from mountebanks. The mantra for retirement accounts, like all invest-ments—diversify—diversify—diversify.

Individual Retirement Accounts, 401Ks, 403Bs, KEOGH
Plans, ROTH IRAs, Company Pension and Profit Sharing Plans, along with others already in place and/or on the drawing board, fall into the category of Tax Sheltered Retirement Accounts. These accounts, with the exception of ROTH IRAs, accept deposits that are deducted from current income before taxes are figured. Earning on these accounts accumulate tax deferred. All these plans fall under the large umbrella called *Qualified Retirement Accounts.*

Taxes on qualified accounts are due, again excepting ROTHs, when money is withdrawn. Tax penalties, currently 10%, are imposed on withdrawals made before age 59ⱼ. Withdrawals must start by age 70ⱼ, or penalties are imposed.

ROTH contributions are not tax-deductible, but earnings are tax-deferred and withdrawals made after 59ⱼ are tax-free. There are currently no withdrawal requirements for ROTH IRAs. Except for ROTHs, qualified retirement accounts work like this:

An individual with $40,000 of income puts $2,000 in a qualified plan and deducts the deposit from income. $38,000 is then used as income when figuring taxes. Taxes on deposits and earnings are deferred until funds are withdrawn. When withdrawn, deposits and earnings are taxed as current ordinary income. The primary advantage of such accounts is they grow faster. They grow faster because earnings that in non-qualified accounts would be used to pay income taxes are reinvested and compounded until withdrawn. A second advantage is many qualified plans may be purchased through payroll deduction plans. Contributions deducted from paychecks avoid the perilous passage around daily wants and wishes. Systematic plans make substantial and meaningful accumulation much more likely.

There are two significant disadvantages to tax sheltered retirement plans. First, once in a tax qualified plan the funds cannot, except under special circumstances, be withdrawn without penalty until the account owner is age 59ⱼ. Early withdrawals are subject to a 10% penalty tax.

Second, when withdrawals are made they are taxed as ordinary income. Assuming a 25% marginal tax rate, a $2,000 annual contribution to an Individual Retirement Account over a twenty-five year period has netted the contributor tax savings on $50,000. Prudently invested for twenty-five years, the account value is likely to exceed $200,000. The account holder has saved taxes on $50,000, but picked up unavoidable tax liabilities for $200,000. There's more. Contrary to popular thinking, the retiree is likely to be in a higher tax bracket when the funds are withdrawn than when they were deposited.

That statement may sound a little strange in light of hype for tax-sheltered accounts, but consider: Deposits are made during child raising, mortgage paying, years when budgets are strained by numerous tax-deductible expenses. Withdrawals are made after these deductions are long past, and have been followed by years of higher earnings. Prime earning years when most people savers save more and put a nice golden shine on the nest egg.

Additionally, those who manage to make regular deposits to tax sheltered accounts are more likely to accumulate other assets and income sources. Those retiring with substantial amounts in qualified retirement plans are unlikely to enter their golden years as poor puppies in low tax brackets. To the contrary, in my experience those with the discipline and foresight to make regular deposits to IRAs usually have more than enough income from other assets. They seldom need the additional *taxable* income.

Which brings us to **ROTH IRAs**, the latest, and for a majority of IRA contributors, the most comely qualified retirement account. Annual deposits of $6000 are allowed for ROTHs.

Taxwise, ROTHs work differently from the other Tax Sheltered Accounts named at beginning of this chapter. ROTH contributions *are not tax deductible, but accumulations are tax-deferred and distributions are tax-free. This often makes* them a very good choice, especially for younger wage earners who can anticipate longer holding periods, or professionals most likely to have longer earning periods and greater wealth accumulation. The longer the holding period the greater the *proportion of earnings to contributions and the greater the value of tax free distribution over tax deductible contributions.*

Unlike most other qualified retirement accounts, ROTH has no withdrawal requirements. As many accumulating substantial amounts in tax sheltered funds do not need them for retirement income, this can be a significant benefit. While other qualified retirement account funds are subject to tax penalties if withdrawals are not started by age 70¡, ROTH funds can pleasingly continue to accumulate untaxed and untaxable, at least under current rules. This untaxed and untaxable income should be not only a great source of pleasure, I say pleasure because few things seem to please the affluent more than tax-free earnings, but can also be used to provide estate liquidity[1]. Fortunately, estate liquidity is often a more important consideration for holders of individual retirement accounts than income.

With all that in mind, let's compare ROTH to a conventional IRA. We use the same twenty-five years of $2,000 contributions as the conventional IRA, assume the account owner paid taxes out of pocket each year and put the same $2,000 in ROTH. After twenty-five years she would have paid taxes on an additional $50,000. We'll pull a number out of the air and assign an average *marginal tax rate* of 25% for the contribution period. This means she has paid $12,500 in taxes over the twenty-five-year period that she would not have paid had the deposits been made to a regular IRA. By paying the $12,500 on the front end, she now is entitled to tax-free distributions from an account worth $200,000. Or, if she doesn't need the money she can just let it grow, penalty free. In this scenario, and from my experience with conventional IRA holders, ROTH looks much better.

In my experience, those who accumulate substantial amounts in tax shelters *are in higher tax brackets at age 70;* when they must begin withdrawals than when they struggled to put the money in. But then, there are worse problems to have at age seventy than excess taxable income.

I recommend moderate use of tax-sheltered accounts, but I also believe it is good to keep an eye on accumulations, and if or when *it becomes obvious that retirement income will be more than adequate, divert savings away from traditional retirement accounts.*

Most retirement plans are too conservatively invested. Investors and investment advisors tend to be too timid, perhaps overly influenced by the disasters that often strike the greedy and/or foolish. Retirement accounts are often considered as investments to be held until retirement. In reality, at retirement, withdrawals may begin, but withdrawals will usually be spread over remaining lifetime. The bulk of the account stays invested and in most cases the amount passing with owner's estate exceeds account value when retirement began. Long-term invest-ments should generally be more aggressively positioned than short-term invest-

---

1.   *Estate Liquidity* refers to proportion of estate is cash or in assets easily converted to cash.

ments. Retirement accounts are for life, about as long-term as we get; for a typical healthy 50 year old, another forty plus years. Keep time in mind when deciding where to invest retirement money.

ESOPs—Employee Stock Option Plans

The substance of this chapter was first published in my column Working Money in the mid-eighties. Post-Enron, few living on planet Earth need this, but history repeatedly proves we learn nothing from history.

The crash of '87, the bubble burst of the nineties and repeated calamities to employees with retirement savings heavily invested in employer stock plans increased general awareness of the peril endemic in failure to diversify. There have subsequently been numerous changes in accounting rules. New regulations have been legislated to protect investors from investment risks. Perhaps those changes will help, but don't bet your retirement on it. And—lest we forget.

The fallacy that government regulations can protect foolish or greedy investors seems to persist despite volumes of evidence to the contrary. Government rules, regulations and law give comfort only to the naive. The wise will seek the security of their own prudence. The maze of convoluted rules *will* increase tax system complexity and create more ways and means to cook books and parboil investors. There is no way to make investing safe from the ministrations of pirates preying on the foolish or greedy without eliminating opportunity for the wise investor.

Through Employee Stock Ownership Plans and other systematic arrangements, individuals often commit large portions of personal savings to stock of a single company. Participating in a company stock purchase plan is an easy way to set money aside, and may be politically advantageous; however, the proportion of each holding should be subjected to frequent review.

Company stock purchases are usually considered retirement investments, and though owning a piece of the company is good, putting too many retirement eggs in one basket could be hazardous to financial health. While prospects for the company may be outstanding, changing times can bring the unexpected. No matter how large or healthy a business, it is vulnerable to the vagaries of time and miscreance, the fickle nature of consumers and government regulation. These uncertainties and the probability of an extended holding period make it wise to spread the risk so personal financial security is not overly dependent on a single enterprise.

Typical investors blanch at the thought of a drop of ten percent in the value of their holdings, but we can come up with many examples where household name stocks have lost half their value in a short period of time. In a diversified portfolio, a loss of value usually precedes a period of exceptional growth; however, with single issues, recovery is less certain, usually takes longer and the loss in value is often much greater.

Holding ten percent of assets in a single stock is considered imprudent for pension or fiduciary plans. They are required to spread investments among companies and investment types because lack of diversification is considered risky. Failure to diversify is riskier for an individual than for pension plans because pensions have many contributors and beneficiaries of varying ages who will draw their money at different times.

I suggest personal assets be reviewed frequently, and if a big chunk of retirement holdings is stock in a single company, a plan for systematic diversification should be considered.

You may not like it—

but if you move your pension you need to know this.

In the new economy job changes are common. Employees, especially professionals and specialists, move around a lot, mostly by choice. When we move, we take our personal pensions such as 401Ks, IRAs or TSAs with us. But, our government doesn't trust us with our pension money. In the ongoing search to make the world foolproof, and perhaps to pick up a tax dollar or two, Congress decided to assume a larger role in managing personal pensions.

HR 5260, mandates a 20% withholding from any pension money passing through the pension owner's hands.

Before the change all we had to do was put it into another qualified plan within sixty days. Under HR6520, the 20% is deducted from pension proceeds, and then, when we put the money back in another retirement account, we must ante up the 20% out of pocket. *After* we put the pension money in another qualified plan, we file for a refund on our next tax return.

What if pocket money's not up to matching the 20% withholding? Well, let's just call it an accelerated tax payment. Anyway, it's for your own good. The idea behind the rule is to protect our pension money from a tendency to spend foolishly what was set aside for our retirement. Foolish spending is something better left to Washington.

If You Move Your Personal Pension

Arrange for the money to be transferred directly between carriers. If this is done, no withholding is required. You can do it yourself or have an agent or broker handle the transaction. If you do it yourself, here's the information needed for a direct rollover.

1.   Name of Plan Sponsor(Previous Employer)

2.   Name/Address of Recipient(Company of your Choosing)

3.   Letter of Acceptance from Recipient

4.   Type of Plan(such as: IRA—401K)

So, you've left International Widget for a new job with Gadget Incorporated. Widget's Office of Human Resources advises you will be receiving $118,227.15 from their pension plan. You're an engineer that knows lots about widgets and gadgets, but not beans about pensions. Don't Panic. Here's what to do.

1.   Contact Widget and tell them: Hold the money pending transfer instructions.

2.   Contact an insurance or investment company and tell them you're moving a pension and need transfer forms.

3.   Complete forms and return to new pension carrier. Notify Widget Human Resources in writing that you are sending transfer instructions.

4.   Send Widget copy of transfer instructions.

Keep copies of your correspondence. Odds are everything will go smoothly, but sometimes there's an error some place, and in spite of your clear instructions *the check arrives in your mail box. If it does, do not deposit, do not endorse, return the check to Widget.*

If you get the check and have copies of correspondence it's usually easy to straighten matters out. If you don't have paperwork, you may be in for a battle, and/or an annoying and troublesome increase in your income taxes.

Now that you are making your own pension decisions what do you do with the money? Best bet. A separate IRA. You are permitted to roll the money into an existing IRA, but if you have occasion to move it again the next transaction is simpler if the money has been held in a separate account.

How should you invest? Here are common choices and their advantages and disadvantages:

Money Market Fund
Advantages: Safety, Liquidity
Disadvantages: Low Yield

Certificates of Deposit
Advantage: Safety, Guaranteed Interest
Disadvantage: Low Yield, Surrender Penalties

Fixed Annuity
Advantages: Safety, Guaranteed Interest, Guaranteed Income Options, Moderate Yields Disadvantages: Annuity Expense, Surrender Charge

Bonds: Advantages: Usually less risky than stock. Moderate Yields Disadvantages: Moderate Risk, Management Requires Specialized Knowledge

Stocks
Advantage: High Yield Potential
Disadvantages: Short-term Risk, Management Requires Specialized Knowledge

Mutual Funds
Advantages: High Yield Potential, Liquidity,
Ease of Management
Disadvantages: Short Term Risk, Fund Expense

Variable Annuities
Advantages: High Yield Potential, Liquidity,
Ease of Management, Income Options
Disadvantages: Short-term Risk, Expenses, Surrender Charges

16

Pension Options—Pension Max?

♦

Dumb as Rocks or Cheatin' Your Spouse

∘ ∘

If we knew what we were doing, it wouldn't be called research.

—Albert Einstein

Summary

One of the biggest decisions many of us face is choosing a pension income option. Pension-max is sobriquet for a scheme where the retiree chooses maximum pension income and provides for a dependent(s) with personally owned life insurance. Choosing a pension option and deciding if Pension Max is good idea is not a complicated process but without a clear understanding of available options and how they relate to needs, the choices can be overwhelming. It is a big-buck decision, one that needs to be carefully made. The most common error in Pension Max calculations is isolating pension benefits from other income. All income sources should be part of the decision. Pension options should be considered as one part of retiree's total financial situation.

Affluent retirees are most likely candidates for Pension Max. Retirees with adequate income and ability to manage personal finances have most to gain from the personal insurance solution. Retirees with marginal incomes or who have difficulty managing personal finances should stick with survivor benefit options.

Pension Max considerations begin with a review of all income and assets. Each of the basic pension options should be plugged into the mix. Pension plans usually offer these options along with a few variations and sub-options.

Pension Max is the name of a scheme where a retiree who needs to provide for a dependent takes Option 1 and provides for the dependent(s) with personally owned life insurance.

Many of the presentations on this question would confuse Solomon and Alan Greenspan. Some retirees are so put off by the confusion they just default to the pension. Not a good idea. The question involves big bucks, often an amount equal to several years income, and well worth the time needed to sort it out.
When we approach the question in a workman-like manner and apply a little logic and common sense, it is not so bad. Answering the following questions gives a basis for considering the numbers:

1. Do retiree and beneficiary have meaningful savings? Personal insurance option leaves retiree and beneficiary with full responsibility for providing beneficiary income should retiree predecease. If no meaningful savings, stick with pension options.

2. Will retirement income exceed needs by comfortable margin? If not, stick with pension options.

3. Is retiree in good health. If not, pension option is probably best.

4. Can beneficiary manage finances? Pension Max leaves beneficiary with management responsibility. If beneficiary is not good money manager stick with pension option.

5. How old is retiree? Pension plan options favor older ages.

6. What is age of beneficiary? The younger the beneficiary, the greater the income reduction for survivor benefits.

7. Will retiree and/or beneficiary earn income after retirement? Post retirement earnings strengthen case for personal insurance.

8. Is beneficiary in poor health? Poor health of beneficiary strengthens Pension Max case.

9. Does retiree or beneficiary own income producing assets? Outside income favors Pension Max.

10. Does retiree own permanent life insurance? Permanent life insurance in force reduces amount of new insurance required to cover survivor benefit.

11. Does beneficiary have separate pension? If so, Pension Max is a more likely choice.

12. Estate tax liabilities a probability? Potential estate tax liabilities favor Pension Max.

Common Pension Options:

Option 1: Life Income Pensioner. Maximum income ending at pensioner's death.

Option 2: Joint and Survivor. Reduced income for lifetime for retiree and beneficiary. Income ranges from roughly 75 to 90% of Option 1, depending on age of beneficiary.

Option 3: Joint, 50% to Survivor. Retiree draws 85 to 95% of Option 1 benefit, depending on age of survivor.

17

Life Insurance & Retirement

o o o o o o o o o o o o o o o o o o o o o o o o o o o o o o o o o

There is one thing stronger…an idea whose time has come.

—Victor Hugo

Summary

During retirement, Life Insurance can be an important source of tax-free income, cash reserves and ultimately, final expenses or estate liquidity. Variable Universal Life policies offer stock and bond options in addition to interest bearing accounts.

The potential for competitive investment returns in combination with life insurance tax advantages make investment oriented policies valuable retirement assets. When you buy life insurance, especially cash value life insurance, you need a good agent. Most are honest and helpful, and it is not difficult to find one you can trust. As with any professional, getting references is a good way to start looking for an agent.

Every profession has charlatans. There are shysters who use knowledge to swindle rather than aid, there are quacks who steal rather than heal and it often seems there's not an honest insurance agent to be found. Although the vast majority of insurance agents are knowledgeable, professionals using their skills to help their clients buy the right policy at a fair price, their image has suffered from too many short timers that that don't know risks from options and can only calculate commissions.

When you buy life insurance, or any insurance product, you need a good agent. Look for one that has been in business for a while. Get referrals from friends and acquaintances. Do the obvious things. But, work with an agent. There are too many places where the difference between knowing and not knowing is critically important. Cash value life insurance is not the least of these places.

Private Pensions

What is a Private Pension? The term "Private Pension" generally refers to a non-qualified retirement account. Non-qualified means contributions are not tax-deductible. Many private pensions use investment oriented life insurance policies as funding instruments because: If a life insurance policy meets Internal Revenue Service guidelines, investment gains are tax-deferred and loans against policy cash values are not taxable income.

Non-qualified private pensions evolved as a result of tax law revisions that have made qualified plans increasingly complex. Lawmakers bent over backwards to prevent pension plans from favoring business owners, high-income executives and professionals. The changing rules made pension administration more difficult at the same time they reduced benefits for owners and managers. Making qualified plans less beneficial and more troublous for pension plan decision makers prompted them to start looking around. They hit on what are not called, 'Private Pensions."

Who can benefit from a Private Pension?

Private pensions are more likely to benefit those with high incomes. Conventional plans such as company pensions, 401ks and Individual Retirement Accounts are adequate for most wage earners. However, qualified plan restrictions and the special needs of highly compensated individuals often make non-qualified alternatives more attractive for those earning high incomes.

In a business, employees who must be included in a qualified plan are a matter of law. With a non-qualified plan, *management decides* which employees participate. This power to determine participants allows companies to reward selected employees in ways that tie them more firmly to the company and gives businesses greater flexibility in designing fringes. The increased control over fringe benefits and the lesser expense of managing non-qualified plans have made them popular supplements to traditional pension plans. Supplements usually offered to a company's key employees.

High income individuals, especially more highly paid professionals and managers, may ultimately find deferring taxes a Pyrrhic victory. Their income tends to grow along with tax rates and they end up paying higher rates on withdrawal. In cases where wealth accumulation is a probability, using life insurance to supplement a traditional pension plan often makes sense.

How do private pensions work? Typically a life insurance policy is purchased on the pensioner. Premiums are paid with after-tax funds at or near maximum deposit levels established by Internal Revenue Service. The high deposit levels build cash value quickly, rapidly reducing the portion of earnings used to pay for term life insurance. At retirement, the untaxed accumulations can be removed by policy loans, which are not taxable. Most high end life insurance policies designed for use as private pensions offer "zero interest" loans. The combination of tax-deferred earnings and tax-free distribution can make investment oriented life insurance a very effective means of providing retirement income. Private pension arrangements are not suited to most wage earners. Those who are unlikely to become financially independent prior to retirement will usually find qualified plans better. If there is a question, finding the best answer usually requires assistance of a financial professional familiar with life insurance and pensions.

Generally, the higher the income and the greater the likelihood of wealth accumulation, the better the odds that a pension oriented life insurance policy will be a good idea. Those who accumulate wealth often have incomes that exceed needs, and unlike most qualified pension plans, life insurance policies have no withdrawal requirements or accumulation penalties.

A note of caution. Private pension proposals rely on life insurance tax preferences to create favorable results illustrated in proposals. These tax advantages are based on historical precedents from times when life insurance profit potential was miniscule and policies were purchased almost solely for death benefits. Some contend newly designed investment oriented policies may be outside the pale of congressional intent and there have been legislative attempts to eliminate some life insurance tax advantages. While these have been unsuccessful so far, there is always the possibility, that future attacks on investment oriented life insurance could be successful. Any private pensions arrangement should consider the potential impact of adverse legislation. It is likely however that should the rules be changed existing policies would be grandfathered.

18

House Rich—Reverse Mortgages

o o o o o o o o o o o o o o o o o o o o o o o o o o o o o o o o

You are a king by your own fireside, as much as any monarch in his throne.

—*Miguel de Cervantes, From* **Don Quixote,**

Summary

A home is often one of retirees' most valuable assets, but one that is seldom considered as a potential source of income. Reverse mortgages can be used to convert home equity to income. Reverse mortgage contracts use mortality tables to project remaining life expectancy and homeowner equity to calculate payments. There is great disparity among contracts, so shop carefully.

Over the years the mortgage balance shrinks and the home appreciates. The house you strained to buy forty odd years ago for $30,000 is now worth $500,000. A cool half-million is just sitting there doing nothing, except giving a warm secure feeling. A warm secure feeling…priceless. But, if called on the house can do more.

Some banks and finance companies will offer a monthly life income in exchange for your home. You retain right of possession and continue to live in the house throughout your lifetime and the reverse mortgage company takes possession at your death.

The income amount depends on property value and remaining life expectancy. The reverse mortgage company expects to make money on the deal. In figuring income amount, or whether to do a deal at all, the mortgage company will consider historical appreciation in the area. A location with a history of increasing property values will get more favorable consideration than one where property values are stagnant or declining.

On entering a reverse mortgage agreement you have sold your home, but retained life possession. Your heirs will not inherit.

19

Single Premium Life

Judgement is not the knowledge of fundamental laws; it is knowing how to apply them.

—*Charles Gow*

Readers may remember when long ago in a time zone far, far away, insurance companies, smarting from regulatory damage to Tax-Deferred annuities, conjured up a new and more effective tax shelter. It was called Single Premium Life. SPL was powerful and it brought in billions of new life insurance premiums. However, if you go there, take care.

Single Premium Life worked like this: The buyer paid a single premium of $5,000 or more for a life insurance policy with the minimum death benefit allowable under Internal Revenue Guidelines. Those guidelines were determined by IRS rules and based on buyer's age and deposit amount.

The deposit, or premium, earned interest or was invested in mutual funds. Because earnings were within the shelter of a life insurance policy they were not subject to income taxes until withdrawn. SPL investments offered policy owners rates of return comparable to ordinary deposits or investments, but tax liabilities were deferred, and with creative management *completely avoidable.* The only disadvantage in a Single Premium Life policy was the cost of life insurance, but that premium was small because the deposit substantially reduces the actual life insurance that is purchased. Taxes on SPL earnings can be avoided by taking loans against policy cash values.

Most SPL policies offer zero interest loans that need not be repaid. Any outstanding loans are deducted from policy death benefits. As readers are probably aware, loan proceeds are not counted as income. So on the bottom line: SPL buyers got life insurance and higher net returns than from other accounts with similar risk levels.

The money flowed in and there was great hoopla, especially in the West where they say everything is grander and the girls oh so pretty, but a little weird. However, all the noise about tax savings flew in the face of Internal Revenue. Tax collectors mounted an assault. After some noteworthy failures a *coup de grace* was delivered by TAMRA.

TAMRA required life insurance premiums to be made in no fewer than five annual installments. If installment rules were violated, the policy would be declared *not life insurance* and any distribution taxed as ordinary income. Single Premium Life was declared dead.

However, the declaration failed to reckon with the ingeniousness of insurance companies, their agents, actuaries, lawyers and other champion schemers. The death knell was premature. Like the Phoenix, single premium life arose from the ashes and is drawing new billions to its wings. Although, shssss…this time everyone's holding down the hoopla.

How is this miracle accomplished? With elegant simplicity. The single deposit is divided between a life policy and an annuity. One-fifth goes directly into the policy and four-fifths into and annuity. The annuity then makes four annual payments to the life policy in a manner that meets IRS guidelines. The scheme complies with the new rules and gives much the same result as original SPLs. The only significant difference is that during the first five years policy owners will have taxable gains from annuity earnings.

As with other insurance, or any scheme for that matter, do some checking. Make sure you get a good contract with a good company and have a good agent to see that the details are right. As a former life agent and financial consultant, I'm probably biased, but I wouldn't get into any investment life insurance without advice of a qualified advisor in whom I had confidence.

20

Your Own Business

♦

I've always wanted to...

o o o o o o o o o o o o o o o o o o o o o o o o o o o o o o o o o o o o o

Almost anyone can make a comfortable living by diligently applying personal skills of hand and mind, but those who can sell others on sharing their goals can do great things—and create important wealth.

—Ayn Rand—Atlas Shrugged

Summary

Professionals and other highly educated persons seldom "retire." As a rule they have too much interest, energy and enterprise to sit back and let the world go by. Seniors that start a new business after "retiring" seem to be the happiest of retirees. And, they have a very high success rate compared to younger entrepreneurs.

When folks are asked what they plan to do after retirement one of the frequent answers is: *I've always wanted to...*

Great, now is the time. Your public and the World need your knowledge, wisdom and experience productively engaged. And, you are better prepared now than ever before to swim in the tricky waters of private enterprise. Your chances for success have been markedly improved by life's lessons. The chances are better than ever before that you will profit financially, physically and emotionally from a later life business venture. Go for it.

It has been my observation that those starting businesses later in life not only have more fun, they also make more money. Going into business is riskier business for the young, probably because they haven't had enough turns around the block. Too often, driven by need, younger entrepreneurs tend to focus on making money right away. Making money right away is not an appropriate goal for a new business. The focus of a business in the early years should be *survival.*

The key to surviving those early years is hard work and self-denial. An advantage of owning your own business is you write your own paycheck. A disadvantage of owning your own business is you write your own paycheck. Too often there's not enough left after everyone else is paid to cover your check.

Besides not being compelled to make quick profits, another reason seniors do better is they get into things they like. When we are doing what we like we work longer, smarter and with greater enthusiasm. When we are happier in our work, we earn more satisfied customers.

You've made the decision to start your own business. What's the next step?

Draw up a business plan:
What are you going to do?
How are you going to do it?
Who will do business with you?
Why will they business with you?
How are you going to promote your business?
How are you going to make money?
How much will your expenses be?
How much money must you make to pay those expenses and show a profit?

Put it together, hard numbers. Be conservative. Now, add a bit to the expense column. Subtract a bit from the revenue line. Sleep on it a day or two. Look over the whole thing again, make needed changes.

If you need or want financing, take your plan to the bank. Your banker may refer you to the Small Business Administration because the loan is a bit too risky for them. If the SBA thinks your business plan is sound and you can put it to work, they will guarantee the loan will be repaid.

Many entrepreneurs seek financial backing from friends or relatives. Be very careful here. A friendship that grows out of a business relationship can be among the best and strongest, but a business relationship that starts with friendship often wrecks both.

You're ready to go. Here are a few tips gleaned from *the experience of others.*

1. Make promises carefully.

2. Keep promises faithfully.

3. Give customers more than they expect.

4. Never take unfair advantage.

5. *When problems arise, assume responsibility.*
    Then ask, what would you like me to do?

6. Be fair to customers.

7. Be fair to employees.

8. Give employees responsibility and trust, but verify.

9. Show appreciation to customers.

10. Show appreciation to employees.
    Be true to those tenets and your business will prosper. It is likely you will soon be doing business with friends and having fun and making money.

◆   ◆   ◆

The experience of others: True stories of private enterprise.

A fledgling retailer had a heavy factory commitment in place when Beanie Baby mania hit. Instead of following others and charging all the market would bear, he kept the price low and used the wildly popular item to build a loyal customer base. He is now a *successful* retailer.

◆   ◆   ◆

The owner of a small electronics manufacturing company often took me on tour of his plant when I stopped by to keep in touch. He would introduce me to employees, tell me about their work and ask them questions.

After a while I tumbled to the fact he was using the tour as a non-confrontational method of keeping in touch with his employees. The *tours* put them at ease and as they told touring strangers about their work the company owner listened carefully. This method helped instill pride and a sense of wellbeing in employees, and the company owner learned important things about his company and his employees.

◆   ◆   ◆

"What we do," says the sole owner of a company developing and manufacturing equipment for the medical field, "is price our products so we can make a fair profit, but not so much as to tempt competitors."

◆   ◆   ◆

"We concentrate on hiring good people, no matter their education or experience," a successful wholesale distributor tells me. "If they are good people we can teach them what they need to know. If they aren't good people, doesn't matter what they know. Once we have them trained, we treat them so well they don't want to go anywhere else."

◆   ◆   ◆

My home air conditioner went out. It was not a cold day in July. It was Mississippi hot. The only thing higher than the temperature was the humidity. With a toddler in the household, a failed air conditioner counted as an emergency. It was the first really hot spell of summer and air conditioners were dying like turkeys at Thanksgiving. Air conditioning repairmen were running weeks behind. Asking one to come right away garnered anything from an amused chuckle to unprintable replies.

Not wanting to go home to a long suffering daughter and a short tempered spouse, I called a friend who owned a flower shop. Flowers wilt quickly in the heat and smart flower shop owners have cooler repairmen on tap. "Do you have someone I could get to fix my air conditioner today?" I asked pleadingly.

"Yes," he replied. "*Al Capone*, he costs, but he comes, and it's fixed when he leaves."

"I'll pay," thinking it would be worth whatever he charged. "Give me the number."

He did, telling me to use his name. I thanked him and hung up.

I called, despaired when I got a machine and left a message without hope.

It was a pleasant surprise when my assistant buzzed me eight minutes later to tell me Al Capone said he could be at my house around eleven this morning to fix the air conditioner.

We had a dog. One conceived when a dog breeder's champion white German shepherd got it on with a neighbor's willing golden retriever. One result of this serendipitous union was a golden gentle giant we adopted and that had become especially protective of our property since his baby girl was born. Even when she was not there, as was the case this morning, he didn't like strangers around. This was nanny's day off and I had left my much doted on daughter at a day care where she had an older boyfriend. He was eleven months. Scary huh?

I called my wife and told her the AC man was coming, do something about Moses, our dog, not the prophet. She put Moses in the back bedroom when she left for class. As I said, it was the nanny's day off but maid's day on. No one had told her why Moses was locked in, so she let him out into our large back yard surrounded with a tall wooden fence.

At eleven fifteen, Al, the air conditioner man called from his truck. Said he was sitting in my driveway. That a really big yellow dog was standing with his head and paws over the gate grinning at him. When he started to get out of the truck the grin changed to a growl and he wasn't getting out of the truck unless we did something about the big yellow dog and he couldn't wait long. I promised to be there in four minutes. By driving the lively Mark VIII aggressively and jumping the long light at the big intersection I made it in three and a half, and was sort of glad to see the truck still in the driveway. I was also glad there was no police car in pursuit. I say sort of glad to see the truck in the driveway because Al was not driving the kind of truck I expected a highly regarded AC man to be driving. In fact it was not a truck I would expect anyone to be *driving*. It looked like a truck that would need to be towed or hauled.

The fenders were multicolored, a strange blue and rust. A big white patch decorated the driver's side door and all the windows I could see were cracked. The truck bed was rounded over with junky looking "stuff" and the springs sagged to the left. As I turned up the drive I could see a trickle of dark liquid staining the concrete.

After I got out of the car and spoke to Moses, Al climbed tentatively out of his truck. He matched his truck to a "T" and I could understand why the truck had been leaning to the left. Al was about average size, for a heavyweight sumo wrestler. It was hard to tell if his ebony face was a racial characteristic or occupational smudge, but his grin exposed a full compliment of super white teeth and convinced me he was friendly.

Obviously this was no effete pretender. Al was what you see is what you get, and I liked him right away. Even with his great size and confident personal bearing Al wasn't going in the yard or the house unless I went with him. So, I did. Moses liked Al, too, and we walked to the big outside unit back on the north side of the house. Al did a few things then diagnosed a bad fan motor. Said he had one on the truck, this will only take a minute.

Fifteen minutes later the air conditioner was cooling away. I was sure it would continue to do so. Despite Al's untidy appearance, and the look of his truck, he inspired confidence. He wrote out a bill. It was a goodly sum but less than I expected.

I said if he wanted to come by the office we could pay him now, but he said had to run, just put the check in the mail. I realized Al trusted me to mail the check because I had been referred by a solid customer. I went back to the office still amused and wondering at Al and his truck. If he stayed busy at the rates he charged one would think he could afford better.

Every day or so I caught myself smiling about that dilapidated looking blue and rust and white truck that leaned to the driver's side and sagged in the rear from the pile in the bed. I never expected to see Al again.

A few months later, on a Thursday afternoon when summer had passed and the weather was cooler I was sitting in my office playing on the internet wondering if it was indecently early to show up at the tennis courts. Corrine, my assistant, buzzed and said Al Capone wanted to see me if he could. Weighing the good service on the air conditioning against the condition of his truck, I figured he had a gambling problem. From his substantial girth I was pretty sure he wasn't on speed, but wanted help figuring out how to pay his bills.

I told Corrine to send him in, already rehearsing the standard line for telling folks they needed someone else for that kind of financial planning. As he lumbered through the door I walked around my desk to shake his huge hand and indicated we should sit at the oak conference table along the wall by the window. As soon as we were seated Al cleared his throat.

"I've got this problem. Thought you might help me." He looked uncomfortable. "Sure Al, what's bothering you?" Certain now that I would need my prepared speech.

"I've got all this money. Don't know what to do with it. Figure there's something better than these." He laid a stack of Deposit Certificates on the table.

A quick glance told me the total would run well into seven figures. It seems that Al with good work and exceptional service had developed a very loyal following. One that was willing to pay premium rates for good and prompt service. Al didn't have a gambling problem, a drug habit or waste money on flashy equipment. He had a highly profitable one man operation. Smart operator. Successful businessman. Life's full of these little surprises. Perhaps someday I'll learn: You can't judge a book by its cover or a man by his truck.

◆   ◆   ◆

Section Four
Estate Planning

o o o o o o o o o o o o o o o o o o o o o o o o o o o o o o o o

It is estimated that between
14 and 18 trillion dollars
will be passed between generations in the next decade.

21

Estate Planning: The Big Picture

Summary

Estate planning is important even for those of modest means. Tax reduction is only one estate planning consideration. Other issues such as providing for equitable asset distribution or business continuation may be of equal or greater importance. For most estates, planning is neither difficult nor costly, but no matter the size or complexity of an estate, failure to plan is almost certain to cause delay, confusion and increased settlement costs. It may also cause estate assets to be distributed without regard for owner's wishes or the best interests of estate beneficiaries.

1. **Failure to plan can wipe out a life's work and leave a bitter family legacy.**

2. **Planning is relatively inexpensive.**

3. **Planning can substantially reduce taxes and other asset transfer costs.**

4. **Most families never get around to it.**

One of the great, and pernicious, myths to come out of recent tax reform legislation is that unless you have mega-bucks there is no need for an estate plan. While it is true that changes in tax law do reduce or eliminate tax liabilities for most small and medium sized estates, it may not happen automatically. And, tax liabilities are only one of a number of important reasons for an estate plan.

It may come as a surprise to many that potential tax liabilities are often not the major consideration in estate planning. Reducing estate taxes is frequently the simplest part of an estate plan. Everyone needs an estate plan. For most, making a will and choosing the right life insurance beneficiaries will do the trick. For others the planning plan will be more complicated, but no matter the size or complexity of an individual or family's holdings, failure to plan can be costly and tragic.

Failure to plan will often result in a distribution of assets completely contrary to owner's wishes and/or the best interests of estate beneficiaries. Failure to plan will almost certainly mean unnecessary delays, increased administrative expense and needless tax liabilities. Additionally, if a family business is involved lack of planning can cause operational disruptions and years of acrimony among family members. It can also make key employees nervous and insecure. Hostile owners and nervous key employees can sink sound companies.

For most families an emotional block stands between them and an estate plan. Estate planning forces contemplation of mortality. It is difficult for most of us to confront that we will someday cease to exist and *that blind worms will fatten on our substance. H*owever, concern for children living and yet unborn should make the issue a priority. The importance of a solid estate plan makes it essential we plow through any hang-ups or holdbacks. Regardless of the size or complexity of an estate it is true that:

1. Failure to plan can wipe out a lifetime's work and leave a bitter family legacy.

2. Planning is relatively inexpensive.

3. Planning can substantially reduce taxes and other asset transfer costs.

4. Most families never get around to it.

Almost everyone has definite ideas for the distribution of their assets, but all too often those wishes are never put to paper. When a property owner dies with the estate plan still in her head taxes, delays, expenses and complications will be maximized. Government coffers and the legal community fare well with head plans but other beneficiaries are not likely to be pleased.

22

Financial Planning to Estate Planning

○ ○

Money you know will hide many faults. Cervantes

Summary

Financial planning and Estate Planning have different objectives. Financial planning seeks to optimize fiscal security of the basic family unit by accumulating and preserving financial assets. Estate planning is devoted to facilitating transfer of assets to an estate's beneficiaries. The most efficient way to transfer assets is to give up ownership or control. Giving away of assets reduces financial security of estate owner. It is useful to understand when the planning focus should shift from financial planning to estate planning.

Most who engage in prudent and thoughtful financial planning accumulate more than will be needed for personal support. When this desirable result comes to pass the primary focus should shift from financial planning to estate planning.

Combining Estate Planning and Financial Planning involves compromise between conflicting objectives: Financial planning focuses on providing maximum financial support and security for estate owner. Estate planning seeks the most efficient transfer of assets to the estate's beneficiaries. The conflict exists because the most expedient method for removing assets from an estate is give it away or put it in trust. Either reduces estate owners' personal wealth and security.

A family financial plan should begin with actions to make the family unit secure against all reasonable risks. This objective should not be compromised, but when it becomes clear that assets will exceed needs, it is time to begin considering how to transfer the excess efficiently.

When shrinkage or costs are mentioned, most think about taxes. Taxes can be devastating, especially when the estate consists largely of highly appreciated illiquid holdings such as a farm or other family business. However, estate values, especially when businesses are involved, may be at risk to greater hazards than taxes. Planning that minimizes or eliminates those hazards is frequently more important than tax reduction. In any event, a sound estate plan can usually do both.

The earlier estate planning needs are considered and the sooner action is taken the better. For most families the accumulation of wealth grows slowly and there will be no obvious signal that estate planning should become a priority. It is therefore prudent to keep an eye on asset growth so planning focus can be shifted. The earlier the process is begun, the better the result.

One of the problems in this neat suggestion is that wealth slips up on most folks. Assets usually grow slowly over time, often to startling amounts without the awareness of those busily making the growth happen. Families often give off the top of their head values that turn out to be a third or a fifth of real worth. Wealth tends to creep up on working folks because they are usually more concerned with making money than counting it. While that is probably healthy from an emotional standpoint, it can be disastrous from an estate planning point of view.

Families should conduct an asset review at least once a year. Sit down, add it up. Get professional estimates or appraisals on real estate and business interests. When the numbers start getting up there, think about increasing the focus on estate planning. Estate planning is almost always a learning experience and, sometimes it's even entertaining. On the other hand, failure to plan can be a hard lesson and no fun at all.

23

Wills & Trusts

✦

No sane person Wants to be a Trustee.

Summary

Many estate owners are so put off by the aura of legal mystique surrounding trusts that they put off estate planning. Trusts are merely instruments directing action and granting authority for that action to an individual or institution. A trust will be as simple or complex as the task it is to perform. Trusts may be revocable or irrevocable. For trust assets to be excluded from an estate, the trust must be irrevocable.

Wills and Trusts are too often steeped in the mysterious mumbo jumbo of lawyer talky and jabberwocky and investment bankas from Sri Lanka. Intimidating monikers *like inter vivos, Charitable Remainder, Eleemosynary, Rabbi…these off putting* sobriquets are simply names given trusts designed for particular purposes. Yet to some they seem to invoke fearful visions of strange places with maps that tell us *don't go there.*

Don't be afraid, Trusts can be elegantly simple things. And, they are essential to good estate planning. They can also be beautiful when *beauty is a function of how beautifully they function.*

Wills and trusts are merely instruments for directing what is to be done with money or property. A will is just what you think it is and a trust is merely an extension of the same idea. Trusts of all stripes are devices property owners may use for directing disposition of assets and they are not by any stretch beyond the comprehension of laypersons.

The different handles have been adopted for the convenience of lawyers, accountants and financial planners. They are no more mysterious than bus, truck or car. Busses, cars and trucks are names of vehicles for transport but each has a different purpose. Like busses, trucks and cars, or apples and oranges, trusts may be for specific purposes or general, i.e. fruit or vehicle. So it is with an *Elee* or a *Rabbi* Trust. A *Charitable Remainder Trust* logically designates a trust form that will pay income to beneficiaries during their lifetime and leave the *remainder* to a designated *charity*.

Trusts may be complicated or simple. Still their function is easily understood and they are simply elegant when smoothing asset transfer and cutting taxes. A trust is an instruction to be carried out either during lifetime or after death. A trustee is entrusted to see to the task. It is said no sane person wants to be a trustee. That is probably true so it's usually smart not to appoint a *person*, but an *institution*.

Trusts may be revocable or irrevocable. The words meaning exactly what they say. A revocable trust may be changed or revoked by during the grantor's lifetime. An irrevocable trust cannot.

Money or property placed into an irrevocable trust is removed from the Grantor's estate because they no longer control the property. Money or property transferred to a revocable trust is still included in the owner's estate for tax purposes because the grantor retains the power to revoke the trust and resume control of the property.

Living Trusts

Living Trusts are also referred to as Revocable Trusts. They are a useful estate planning tool. However some marketing methods have created justifiably skepticism. Like Variable Universal Life and tax-sheltered this or that, Living Trusts caught the fancy of snake oil salesmen and have been misused.

Don't let the problems dissuade you from the concept if it seems to fit. There are many valid uses for Living Trusts, AKA *inter vivos*. Property in a Living Trust at death of grantor avoids probate. Avoiding probate can be advantageous. Avoiding probate can reduce settlement time, legal expenses and avoid public disclosure. However, *Living Trust property is subject to estate taxes.*

Avoiding probate is not always desirable. There are times when beneficiaries, minor children, for example, who may benefit from probate court administration.

Living trusts have been widely offered as a way to save money by avoiding paying a lawyer. There are times when you really do need a lawyer. When you need a lawyer or any other advisor, it is cheaper to pay for their services than to go it alone.

I know a lot of lawyer jokes and have known shysters that fit the image. But, lawyers are like insurance agents, financial planners, bankers, physicians, used car salespersons…some are better than others. When you are considering a trust of any hue, you need a reliable financial and legal advisor. Or, or you can spend a few months or years of dedicated study to bone up on the subject, but you probably have better things to do. My physician is pretty darn smart, but he can't fix my car, come to think of it, neither can my mechanic. In designing a trust to fit your unique needs, you should have a reliable lawyer and a good lawyer and a good financial advisor. A trust without a trusted financial advisor and a lawyer—don't go there.

24

Doing Well By Doing Good

◆

Charitable Remainder Trusts

○ ○
My Candle burns at both ends,
it will not last the night,
but oh my foes, and ah, my friends,
it gives a lovely light.

—*Edna St. Vincent Milay*

Summary

A Charitable Remainder Trust pays life-time income to beneficiaries. After death of beneficiaries, the remainder value passes to the designated charity. A Charitable Remainder Trust is useful in converting highly appreciated assets to income without paying taxes on the appreciation. It can also facilitate buying and selling investments to increase diversification without triggering tax liability for gain.

Most individuals who accumulate wealth in excess of immediate family needs have specific objectives for their estates. As a rule, these folks have a serious preference for enjoying fruits of their labor, disinheriting the Internal Revenue Service and leaving a little something to a favorite charity. It can happen even in our imperfect world.

An often overlooked estate planning tool with the intimidating sobriquet Charitable Remainder Trust (CRT) can be helpful. Don't be put off by the heavy name, CRTs are relatively simple. The trust grantor transfers assets to the CRT. The trust manager (trustee) invests those assets, pays a lifetime income to the donor and donor's spouse. At death of beneficiaries, the trustee turns remaining trust assets over to the designated charity.

Simple, yes—*but oh, my foes and, ah my friends, it gives a lovely light.* CRT's are loved by charities and estate planners because they do good things and ax taxes while they do good things. Estate owners often have highly appreciated assets such as stocks or real estate that produce little or no current income. It is often advantageous to sell those assets and convert the proceeds to income but tax liabilities on appreciation may make the conversion impractical.

Also those highly appreciated assets may be closely held stock in one or two companies. It would be prudent to diversify to reduce business risk. But again, potential taxes on appreciation are obstacles to prudence.

A CRT can solve both problems. When appreciated assets are transferred to a CRT, capital gains tax is avoided and the entire transferred value is available to produce income. Additionally, the trust manager can buy and sell stock held in the CRT to increase diversification without triggering tax liabilities.

Estate taxes are reduced when the assets are removed from the estate. The transfer also creates deductions against current and future income.

But horrors, estate values are reduced and you wanted to leave it all to the ungrateful kids. Here's to having your cake and eating it too. So long as the estate owner's health is reasonably good, part of the trust income would be used to buy life insurance owned by a Wealth Replacement Trust replace what was transferred to the CRT.

Family Charitable Trusts

Most charitable trusts are through established charities or institutions such as a university. These are simple and effective, the institution does the work and bears the legal expense. Institutional CRTs are heavily promoted by their sponsors and get the most exposure. However, many extended families have a common cause and might elect to establish a Charitable Remainder Trust to serve that cause. For example: An extended family might have a strong interest in promoting education or preserving the environment. They might also be in a position to benefit from a Charitable Remainder Trust that could also support for their special interest.

For example: The descendents of Dick and Jane Smith are spread far and wide. They are generally successful. They are generally successful because the family has a long tradition of encouraging education.

A disproportionate number of Dick and Jane's descendents are teachers and they would like to support for the educational process by encouraging more college students to become teachers.

Dick and Jane are comfortable and have a meaningful sum they could contribute to such a project. They also run the idea by their successful children and grandchildren. The younger generations like the idea and a family trust is designed to assist college students pursuing degrees in education. Many of Dick and Jane's descendants will qualify for financial aid under the terms of the trust.

The Smith Family Educational Trust offers the Smiths, and anyone else wanting to participate, the same benefits as a Charitable Remainder Trust sponsored by an institution, but, one that specifically addresses family concerns. The disadvantage of a family trust is start up and administrative expenses.

25

Life Insurance & Estate Planning

Summary

Life insurance can provide cash to pay estate taxes, debts and facilitate equitable distribution of assets. Proceeds of life insurance on an estate holder that is owned by others, such as irrevocable trusts or estate beneficiaries, is not subject to estate taxes. Life insurance ownership is transferable. Existing life insurance policies can be removed from an estate by transferring ownership to other estate beneficiaries or to an irrevocable trust. Trusts or estate beneficiaries may purchase life insurance on the estate owner. Estate owners can make gifts to estate beneficiaries for payment of life insurance premiums.

Many sizeable estates are heavy in property and light in cash. Death of an estate owner almost always brings need for cash to pay taxes, settle debts and tie up loose ends. Land or business interests sold to raise cash are almost certain to bring much less than true value.

Farm land and other business interests are especially vulnerable to shrinkage. In addition to the devaluation inherent in a forced sale there is the possibility for costly business disruptions. There may also a problem selling the shares of a closely held company. Is a competitor likely to pay fair market value to *buy your business?*

It is also likely that in a family owned business, ownership needs to remain in hands of key employees for the business to remain profitable, or even viable. When a business is a substantial part of an estate, life insurance proceeds can provide for equitable distribution to estate beneficiaries not involved in the business without disturbing business ownership.

For Example: Four children are beneficiaries of an estate. Two are active in the business and two are not. The interests of those active in the business may conflict with the interests of those that are not. Life insurance policies insuring estate owners and owned by the business may be used to buy inherited stock of estate beneficiaries with no active interest in the business. A buy and sell agreement among the parties should be used to spell out the details.

Life insurance is property, and as with other forms of property, that ownership is transferable. Most estate owners will have purchased life insurance throughout their lifetimes. If they *own* these personal policies, the policy proceeds will be included in their taxable estate. Proceeds of these policies can be removed from the estate by transferring ownership to estate beneficiaries or to a life insurance trust.

When policy ownership is transferred there is a period, currently three years, during which the policy proceeds will be pulled back into the estate. For the first three years after transfer, the IRS considers property transfers as action taken in *anticipation of death*. After the anticipation death has passed, life insurance proceeds will not be a part of the insured's estate.

A trust may buy life insurance direct. The trust should be named as policy *applicant and owner*. When the trust buys the policy, so long as the trust is irrevocable, the policy is not a part of the estate. The estate owner may transfer funds to the trust to pay life insurance premiums.

Estate beneficiaries may also buy life insurance on estate owners. Gifts from the estate to beneficiaries may be used to pay life insurance premiums. The gifts may utilize the Annual Exclusion or the Unified Gift Tax Credit. So long as the policy is owned, and premiums are paid by, an entity other than the estate owner, policy proceeds will not be part of the taxable estate.

26

Family Corporations &
Partnerships

Summary

Family Corporations and Partnerships are excellent estate planning tools. They can provide be useful for organizing and transferring business interests. Family Corporations and Partnerships can permit estate owners to retain control of a company or property while transferring the majority of a company's value to others.

A business is usually started by and individual with a number of special skills. The profitability of the company often depends on continued availability of those special talents.

The combination of ability and determination needed to start and manage a profitable business is rare, and without careful planning, most family businesses will die with their creator. When the founder dies, the business loses the skill and creative drive that built the company. Additionally, the founders often retain ownership throughout their lifetimes and at their death ownership may pass to others who do not fit harmoniously into the operation.

Suppliers, creditors, and customers can become uneasy about the company's future. Their concerns can disrupt cash flow and strain liquidity. When ownership passes to individuals not involved in the company, new owners may be more interested in distributions than operations. This difference in priorities can put new owners in conflict with key employees, who lacking real authority, may fear for their jobs and be tempted to seek less shaky ground.

A combination of management turmoil and financial strain can sink a prosperous company. These problems, though serious, can usually be overcome with thoughtful planning. Unfortunately, most business owners never get around to putting such a plan in place.

Every business is unique. As unique as it's founder, and so every business plan will be different, but a couple of examples may be helpful.

The Family Corporation

Alfred Carlotti started ABC Company in his garage twenty-five years ago. He had nothing but and idea and borrowed against his home for start up capital. Today, Mr. Carlotti is sixty. Under his guidance ABC has enjoyed steady growth and now has 200 employees. He is proud of the company and wants do what he can to make sure it is preserved for his family and employees.

Mr. C still runs the company and owns all the stock. He has three children; two are professionally employed and have no interest in the family business. The third, Sara Caroltti, age thirty, works at ABC and expects to take over at Mr. C's retirement.

Mr. C is concerned about what might happen to the company in the event of his untimely death or disability. He is pleased by Sara's interest in ABC and has confidence in her ability. He wants the company to pass to her but thinks it will be several years before she's ready to run the company. Carlotti believes key employees could keep the company going until his daughter is ready to assume leadership, but nonetheless is concerned about what could happen if he were taken out of the picture in the near future.

To improve his company's chance for survival, he draws up a plan to retain key employees and to make sure money will be available to help the company to operate efficiently.

First, he determines the company has five *Key Employees*. His daughter, Sara, and four others are essential to profitable operations. An agreement is entered which obligates Mr. C's estate to sell and these employees to buy 80% of ABC stock at Mr. C's death. Sara will buy 60% and the other key employees 5% each. Each key employee buys life insurance on Mr. C sufficient to fund their stock purchase. The company will make loans to employees for payment of insurance premiums. The premium loans will be secured by policy cash values.

Alfred Carlotti's plan greatly improves the company's chances for surviving his premature death. At the same time it ties employees critical to the company's profitability more firmly to ABC. Under the plan Sara will have the controlling interest of ABC, Incorporated when her father dies.

The Family Limited Partnership

Family Limited Partnerships (FLP) have been around for awhile. But, much to ire of IRS, they have recently become central to a hot new estate planning strategy. This strategy uses FLPs to transfer ownership of family assets to younger generations while leaving elders in charge of operations and in control of the lion's share of income.

The Limited Partnership consists of a General Partner(s) and limited partners. The general partner(s) is active manager and has total authority over company operations. In addition to a share of profits, general partners usually are paid salaries and expenses. Limited partners share profits but have no say in company management. This neat division of ownership and operating authority can make the Family Limited Partnership a very efficient business arrangement, and a useful estate planning tool. Let's take an example:

Mom and Pop have a profitable little company valued at one million dollars. They have two children and four grandchildren. They divide the business into one hundred partnerships valued at $10,000 each. There create two general partnerships, one for Mom, one for Pop, and ninety-eight limited partnerships. Under this arrangement, Mom and Pop, as general partners, retain total control of the company, irrespective of ownership of the ninety-eight limited partnerships.

Mom and Pop are paid salaries and expenses for running the business. After salaries and operating expenses are deducted from income, profit is divided equally among the 100 partnerships. Every year after the FLP is established, Mon and Pop gift shares to children and grandchildren using the $10,000 per person *annual gift tax exclusion.*

Between them they can give $20,000 worth of shares to *each beneficiary* every year. Share values can be discounted for such factors as limited marketability and minority interest. Tread carefully here, but with the aggressive discounting some advisors suggest, transfer values could be reduced to as little as $5,000 per share.

With their combined annual gift exclusion limit, Mom and Pop are able to remove 98% of the company's value from their estates in just a few years. And, if desirable, the transfers can be accelerated by using unified gift tax credits. Within careful limits, a good CPA needed here, management techniques and expenses can be varied to direct more or less income to general partners in salaries and expenses.

The Family Limited Partnership is an excellent financial planning tool, but FLPs are coming under increased scrutiny and it is the better part of wisdom to make sure that any Family Limited Partnership that reduces estate tax liabilities has a *defensible business purpose,* a business purpose *other* than reducing taxes.

Section Five
Odds & Ends

o o o o o o o o o o o o o o o o o o o o o o o o o o o o o o o o o o o o

A government that robs Peter to pay Paul can always depend on the support of Paul.

—*G. B. Shaw*

27

Paying For College—A Million Dollar Baby

Summary

When students apply for financial aid the family's financial condition is usually considered in determining awards. All assets are not treated equally. Cash, stocks and bonds, even college savings plans, may reduce eligibility for aid. Other equally valuable holdings, such as home equity, life insurance cash values or annuity holdings, are seldom used to reduce awards. Check with financial aid department of prospective colleges and meet with your financial advisor to review your asset structure as it relates to future college financial aid.

When students apply for financial aid, family wealth is considered in determining amounts awarded. Assets, especially liquid assets, such as cash, stocks and bonds usually reduce eligibility; however, all assets are not treated equally. Life insurance cash values, annuities and home equity are seldom counted. Ownership of these assets does not normally reduce aid amounts.

Ironically, accumulating funds in a college savings account will usually shrink the aid package. Depending on tax considerations, rather than setting up a college savings plan, one might do better to pay down the home mortgage and plan on a home equity loan for college expenses. There are other more interesting possibilities, but I have a healthy reluctance to put them in print.

The currents in these waters are swift and rather than be more detailed, I suggest checking with the financial aid section of prospective colleges while college bound offspring are in advanced potty training. With the financial aid office's information packet in hand, make an appointment with your financial advisor and review the efficacy of different arrangements. Keep in mind when planning your college funds that, like all things involving money and life—change is inevitable. Looking ahead and staying flexible will yield better results.

On the lighter side, if you have, or are contemplating, children, the following might be of more than passing interest. Playing with numbers from a recent government study indicates the cost of raising a single child in a middle income family could exceed One Million Bucks. Ridiculous, well, it *was* a government survey, but let's examine the issue.

Those thinking of that first child probably have given some thought to major expenses, like prenatal and hospital care...$3000—5000 my sources say, and maybe another grand or so to fix up a nursery. Reasonable estimates, and certainly within the ball park, but those are not the major expenses, just the small beginnings.

One survey, performed by government economists, indicates a first child absorbs one-fourth a family's income. That fourth, conservatively invested over a twenty-five year period should yield a bit over seven figures. Scary. Think of the bass boats, golf clubs and tennis shoes that money could buy.

It could be worse, if your child is gifted or talented, and how could it be otherwise, you will want to provide every opportunity for the little critter to develop their blessings. Gifted or talented raises the ante. *World Tennis* magazine recently told us that, starting at age eleven, raising a talented tennis player, with lessons, equipment and travel for competition can easily exceed $25,000 a year. Worse still, your kid could be academically and/or musically gifted. In that case the cash outflow starts earlier and lasts longer.

The luckiest parents could end up helping repay education loans with their retirement checks. And if the real cost of raising kids gets out, there could be a dearth of kids. There might not be enough youngsters around to pay into Social Security what we're taking out.

Take heart, prospective parents. The second child is much cheaper, and with the third or fourth, they say you hardly notice the expense, or anything else. Another thing, don't let's take these numbers too seriously: The twenty-five percent figure came from government sources, maybe the same sources that prompted the aphorism, I'm *from the government and I'm here to help you.* No doubt, kids are a great impediment to wealth, but as discussed before, lot'sa money won't make you nearly so rich as children and grandchildren.

28

The Best Investment

o o o o o o o o o o o o o o o o o o o o o o o o o o o o o o o o
Only the educated are free. Epictetus.

Summary

People often ask about low risk investments that have high return potential. The general rule is returns are proportionate to risk. Investments with high return potential are risky, and safe investments don't make much. Usually, investment offerings touting low risk and high returns should be deposited in file thirteen along with offers of government help. However, there seems to be an exception.

My skepticism about low risk/high yield investments was challenged recently when one of my clients put me onto an investment scheme that has no risk and very high return potential. Such representations call for extreme skepticism, but because my source has exceptional credibility, I checked this one out. Here's what I found.

Of those willing to discuss the matter, none regretted their investment, indeed nearly all wished they had more, and most indicated that while the financial returns exceeded expectations, ancillary benefits proved more valuable. I normally try to avoid burdening readers with numbers, but this investment has such a strong performance history and so many recommendations, that an exception is in order. According to my sources, $26,000 yielded an average return of $528,000 and a $50,000 investment returned $1,571,520.

The difference is not pure profit because in addition to money, this investment requires contributions of time and effort. Sweat equity, if you will. However, those who would talk about this investment believed they benefited from the extra work.

What could be so great and not make headlines 'round the world, or at least The Money Times or Twenty Minutes?

The investment referred to is *EDUCATION*. The cost and average earnings were drawn from World Almanac. The numbers given reflect the additional career earnings of college graduates over high school graduates and post graduate degree versus a high school diploma. Also, those finishing high school earned $400 a month more than those who did not.

It is expected earnings gaps will widen in the future. As society becomes more complex, greater skill will be required to perform the world's work and the value of knowledge will increase as technology makes distribution of information faster and easier. The value of knowing and the cost of not knowing will grow.

We are facing a future of accelerating change. This change offers both carrot and stick. Those with the ability to get things done will become more valuable. They will be rewarded with money, prestige, and a wide range of career and lifestyle options. Others will find fewer jobs, and those jobs will pay less.

The poorly educated will find it difficult to keep up with new methods and be increasingly relegated to less rewarding routine tasks, or worse still, they may become unemployable wards of a government less and less capable of managing their support. The handwriting is on the wall. It reads, those who know will do well, and those who don't know will do without.

It should be made clear that *education* refers not merely to what the young do in school, growing educated is a never-ending journey. A diploma or degree is not the end of an educational process, merely a jump start beginning. Those without diplomas or degrees can catch up, but they will find it more difficult to get into the race, and then they must run faster. The biblical story of talents seems to apply: It's not what you have, it's what you do with what you have.

My work has brought me in contact with a wide range of people; most are financially well to do, and most are well educated. If I were to create an index for measuring personal satisfaction and well being, education would rank at the top of the scale. Money doesn't seem to be a big factor. Investing in education is a no brainier; the educated make more money, they lead richer lives, and after all, *"Only the educated are free."* Epictetus

Epilogue

One of our most enduring myths is the idea that the elderly are poor. Our elderly are far richer than our youngsters. The elderly are poor or rich for the same reasons young folks are poor or rich: Education, initiative and ambition. This is likely to be even more certain in the future.

Knowledge is the ticket, not only to wealth, but to options. As the world becomes richer, and hopefully our capacity for delivering the fruit of our bounty improves, even the poorest among us should have plenty. Options, however, are the important ticket to those elusive, difficult to define attributes of *happiness and wellbeing.*

Education most of all creates options that allow us to choose work, locations and lifestyles that suit us. Those without education will have fewer options and increasingly be stuck doing what they must. The best educated will do more as they please.

We are faced with three certainties in the near future.

One: The educated human will become too valuable for manual labor. Manual labor will be increasingly performed by machines as we build them smarter and more agile. Those without education will be left out.

Two: The affairs of all people and countries are inextricably linked. Time, technology and scientific advances will increase the complexity and closeness of that linkage. The world's borders will become less and less meaningful and our financial well being will be affected not only by our personal decisions, but also by decisions made in Washington, London, Tokyo or Kuala Lumpur. It is important that our personal plans give due consideration to international events and trends as well as goings on here at home. This smaller world syndrome will continue at an exponentially increasing pace.

Three: We will live longer, much longer. All the experts agree. How much longer, there the experts diverge. The conservatives put the upper limit at 125 healthy vigorious years. The far outs say molecular biologists will eliminate disease and againg as a cause of death and that there is no upper limit on human lifespans.

If these posits are true, as I believe they are, financial planning to create options that make our lives happier and better becomes even more important. Lifestyle options become more important because we will live with them much longer. More reasons to buy, read and use this book.

◆   ◆   ◆

Although the United States is still one of the best places in the world to do business, it still seems at times that legislative activity is our greatest handicap. *Trade and commerce, if they were not made of India rubber, would never manage to bounce over the obstacles which legislators are continually putting in their way; and, if one were to judge these men wholly by the effects of their actions and not partly by their intentions, they would deserve to be classed and punished with those mischievous persons who put obstructions on the railroads.*[1] Good argument can be made for a moratorium on regulatory change. Our legislators posture and pontificate, but in the end do little to effect meaningful change, or damage their chances of re-election.

Comes to mind the Oriental Blessing/Curse: *May you live in interesting times.* But then, how could our times not be interesting? We live in the beginning of a new millennium, proximate time to the worst terrorist attack in U. S. history. And, we live on the cusp of a communications revolution that will ever more rapidly change the way we live and work. The world is moving at an exponentially increasing pace. It is carrying us to places even the most visionary seers could not have imagined at the end of the twenty-first century.

As I write this, we are embroiled in another war. Hopefully, this war will be the last, but we read others are *planned.* Even the threat of war is a setback. Threats of war do damage to our personal and financial security. As ever, it seems we move forward some, then slide back a bit. Still, I believe we will solve our problems and move on, hopefully learning new ways to make the world a gentler, more nurturing, place. Perhaps we could even learn to benefit from our differences rather than make war over them.

---

1.   Civil Disobedience—Thomas Jefferson or Thoreau? Check t his...

It seems those of us born in the twentieth century are enamored of our knowledge; yet, I suspect, what we've learned might be likened to a bucket of water dipped from a great ocean. *We've come a ways, but we ain't seen nothing' yet.* We cannot imagine what lies beyond the horizon, or how our lives and our fortunes will be molded by what we find there.

We are fortunately born. I suppose, given the complex, convoluted and dangerous events our ancestors navigated to reach our conception, any birth is fortunate, but those of us living in this tumultuous third millennium, are among the world's most blessed. With prospects limited only by our imagination and willingness to go for it, we need only prepare. With *the democratization of education*[2] and the capacity of the Internet to share and distribute information, we need only pluck knowledge, our tickets to prosperity, from cyberspace.

Education, though is more than acquiring knowledge, it is also—learning to think. Smart people often believe dumb things. Many believe in astrology, others in *Creation Science* or *Intelligent Design*. And, according to a recent National Science Foundation report, a majority of college graduates believe magnetic therapy works.

Intelligent people hold nonsensical beliefs not from lack of knowledge, but due to a failure to think critically. It is said, *Those who know nothing can be led to believe anything.* Makes sense, but it seems those who don't think about what they learn aren't much better off. Knowledge without thinking is like a fine automobile without fuel: ; it looks good and will roll downhill, but it won't take you to new highs. Thinking is fuel for putting knowledge to work. So, our challenge for financial planning and for living: learn, then think about it.

Tolerance is essential to freedom. Without tolerance for differences in race, beliefs and lifestyles that exist in the diverse community of man, society will always be straining to repair the ravages of conflict. Terrorist bombings around the world have provoked rage and an international war on terrorism. Unless we are prudent, our war on terrorism will unduly compromise freedom of all the world's citizens.

Terrorists aim to provoke fear and violence. If we rail against others who look, dress or think differently, we amplify the conflicts terrorists design to create. In adjusting to new-world realities, we must be careful of our fears and vigilant of

---

2.   The Bell Curve, Charles Murray & Richard Herrnstien

our liberty. Otherwise we may hand terrorists their ultimate victory by making ourselves prisoners of our own fear and intolerance with hastily drawn laws that free people everywhere should find intolerable. Tolerance, because it's a small, small world. As _____ advises, *Those who choose safety over freedom are destined to lose both.*

TLSacristen

Glossary

Acid Test Ratio: The value of company assets divided by its liabilities.

Annual Exclusion Allowance: Annual tax-free gift allowance.

Annual Report: Public Corporation's annual report to shareholders.

Annuitant/Joint Annuitant: Income beneficiary of an annuity.

Asset: Something of value.

Balance Sheet: Financial statement. Total of assets, capital and liabilities.

Beta: Index of price volatility of a stock compared to similar stock.

Book Value: Net worth divided by number of outstanding shares.

Broker: Person or agent that buys and sells stocks and bonds.

Capital Gain: Profit from sale of assets.

Capital Gains Tax: Tax on capital gain.

Cash Flow: Income and Expenses. One index to company's financial health.

Certificates of Deposit: Popularly called "CDs". Account with rate of interest guaranteed for a specific period.

CFA: Certified Financial Analyst. Financial Specialist

CFP: Certified Financial Planner. Financial Planning Specialist.

ChFC: Chartered Financial Consultant. Financial Planning Specialist.

CLU: Chartered Life Underwriter. Life insurance specialist.

Compound Interest Rule: Also called Rule of 72. 72 divided by compound interest rate equals number of years in which principal will double.

CPA: Certified Public Accountant. Tax and accounting specialist.

Current Assets: Assets that can be converted to cash within one year.

Depreciation: Deduction allowed for asset that loses value.

Dollar Cost Averaging: Investing set amounts at regular intervals and theoretically benefiting from fluctuations in share prices.

Earnings Per Share: Net income divided by outstanding shares of common stock.

Estate Tax: Tax on assets owned at death.

Fixed Assets: Property not quickly convertible to cash.

Golden Handcuffs: Benefit package tying employee to a company.

Grandfathered: In Contracts, subject to laws in effect at time of inception.

Grantor: Person who makes grant.

Guideline Maximum Insurance Premium: Maximum life insurance premium allowed for policy to have life insurance tax treatment.

Intestate: Without a valid will

Joint Tenancy: Form of ownership where two or more persons have undivided interest in the entire property.

Key Person: Valuable employee whose loss would diminish company profitability.

Limited Partnership: Legal entity consisting of General and Limited Partners.

Living Trust: Revocable Trust arrangement often used as Will.

Living Will: Instruction regarding terminal health care.

LUTCF: Life Underwriter Training Council Fellow. Life insurance specialist.

Marginal Tax Rate: Tax rate on last dollar earned.

Marital Deduction: Allows unlimited transfer of estate assets to a spouse.

National Association of Insurance Commissioners: Oversees U. S. Insurance Matters

Non-qualified Accounts: Deposits to non-qualified accounts are *not tax-deductible*.

Overfund: Exceed life insurance premiums required to support life insurance policy benefits.

Per Stirpes: Method of dividing estate whereby a deceased heir's descendents share their ancestor's portion.

Period Certain: Annuity Guaranteed Income Period.

Policy Loan: Loan against life insurance cash value.

Private Corporation: Stock not sold publicly. Stock owned by a family or a few unrelated individuals.

Private Pension: A non-qualified private retirement plan. Usually a Maximum Premium Variable Universal Life or Single Premium Life policy.

Probate Court: Judges validity of a will and oversees administration of estate.
Prospectus: Describes stock, mutual fund or investment offering.

Qualified Retirement Account: Deposits are tax deductible and withdrawals taxable as income. Roth IRA is an exception.

Roth IRA: Deposits made with after tax income. Withdrawals are tax free.

Reinsurance: Insurance purchased by an insurance company to protect against catastrophic loss.

Rule of 72: Also called Compound Interest Rule. 72 divided by compound interest rate equals number of years required for principal to double.

Stock Index: A representative group of stock such as the Dow Jones or S&P 500.

Transfer at Death: Provision whereby change of ownership is triggered by death of contract holder.

Unified Gift Tax Credit: Deductible from an estate before taxes are figured.

Wash Loan: Or Wash *anything*. A loan or transaction in which there is no loss or gain.

Wealth Replacement Trust: Trust established to receive life insurance proceeds as replacement for assets transferred out of an estate.

Whole Life: Also called Straight Life. Life insurance policy with level premium.

Yield: Dividend expressed as fraction of share value.

978-0-595-28134-3
0-595-28134-6

www.ingramcontent.com/pod-product-compliance
Lightning Source LLC
Chambersburg PA
CBHW030756180526
45163CB00003B/1047